Editor
Erica N. Russikoff, M.A.

Managing Editor
Mara Ellen Guckian

Illustrator
Mark Mason

Cover Artist
Brenda DiAntonis

Editor in Chief
Ina Massler Levin, M.A.

Creative Director
Karen J. Goldfluss, M.S. Ed.

Art Coordinator
Renée Mc Elwee

Imaging
Rosa C. See

Publisher
Mary D. Smith, M.S. Ed.

Third Grade SUCCESS

Reinforce and review standards-based skills

Across-the-Curriculum Activities

LANGUAGE ARTS

MATH

SOCIAL STUDIES

SCIENCE

INCLUDES

BONUS Language Arts and Math activities to get a jump start on Fourth Grade!

Author

Susan Mackey Collins, M.Ed.

Teacher Created Resources
6421 Industry Way
Westminster, CA 92683
www.teachercreated.com

ISBN: 978-1-4206-2573-8

© 2011 Teacher Created Resources
Made in U.S.A.

Teacher Created Resources

Table of Contents

Introduction

Each time a student enters a new grade, he or she is excited to begin a new curriculum and master the plethora of brand-new and challenging skills that come with that grade. All students are intrigued when they learn something new. Remember how fun it was when you learned to write cursive letters for the first time? Or what about the first time you conducted an experiment in the science lab? How exciting it was to see if your experiment would go the way you had planned!

Third Grade Success is part of a series that reminds each one of us how wonderful and exciting it is to advance to a new grade. Although each grade contains required fundamentals that all students need to master, one must not forget that learning itself, no matter the skill, is exciting. *Third Grade Success* helps instill the fundamentals each student will need to be successful academically; it also captures a student's imagination and love of learning as he or she completes each skill and is ready to move on to the next one.

All lessons in the series meet the national standards required by today's most innovative teachers. Activities in this book are perfect for the classroom teacher but can also be utilized by parents hoping to offer extra practice outside of the classroom. Teachers and parents can select pages that will provide additional practice of a concept, or they can choose pages to teach new concepts. *Third Grade Success* includes skills in the following areas:

- **Language Arts**   • **Math**   • **Social Studies**   • **Science**

An answer key is provided for these pages beginning on page 168.

Third Grade Success has a special bonus section at the end to provide a jump start for fourth-grade skills. Bonus sections are provided at each level in the series. As teachers and parents work through the skills in each book, they can easily move on to the next grade level whenever they feel a student is ready. For the regular classroom teacher who has just finished with state testing, this extra section will help ensure all students are moving forward. This bonus section has its own answer key beginning on page 191.

Have a successful year!

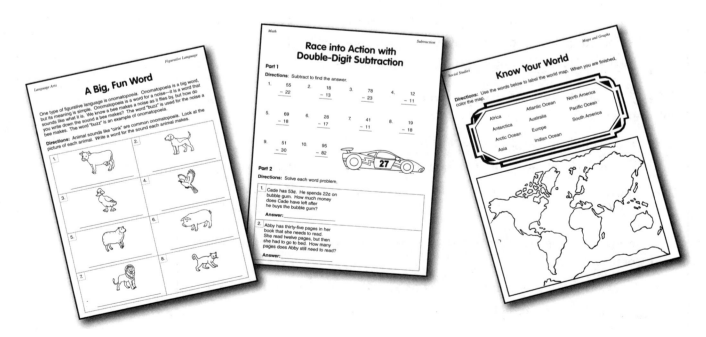

Meeting Standards

Each lesson in *Third Grade Success* meets one or more of the following standards, which are used with permission from McREL. (Copyright 2010 McREL. Mid-continent Research for Education and Learning. Telephone: 303-337-0990. Website: *www.mcrel.org/standards-benchmarks*)

Language Arts Standards and Benchmarks	Page Numbers
Uses grammatical and mechanical conventions in written conventions	
• Writes in cursive	8–35
• Uses nouns in written compositions	36–38
• Uses verbs in written compositions	39–41
• Uses adjectives in written compositions	42
• Uses adverbs in written compositions	43
• Uses conjunctions in written compositions	44
• Uses negatives in written compositions (avoids double negatives)	45
• Uses conventions of spelling in written compositions	48, 60
• Uses conventions of capitalization in written compositions	49–50
• Uses conventions of punctuation in written compositions	51–57
Gathers and uses information for research purposes	
• Uses key words, guide words, alphabetical and numerical order, indexes, cross-references, and letters on volumes to find information for research topics	47
Uses the general skills and strategies of the reading process	
• Uses phonetic and structural analysis techniques, syntactic structure, and semantic context to decode unknown words	46
• Understands level-appropriate reading vocabulary	59–60
• Understands the author's purpose or point of view	61, 65
Uses reading skills and strategies to understand and interpret a variety of literary texts	
• Understands the basic concept of plot	62, 63, 64
• Understands the ways in which language is used in literary texts	66–69
• Knows the defining characteristics of a variety of literary forms and genres	58, 70–71
Uses reading skills and strategies to understand and interpret a variety of informational texts	
• Knows the defining characteristics of a variety of informational texts	72–73
• Summarizes and paraphrases information in texts	74

Meeting Standards *(cont.)*

Math Standards and Benchmarks	Page Numbers
Understands and applies basic and advanced properties of the concepts of numbers	
• Understands the basic difference between odd and even numbers	75
Uses basic and advanced procedures while performing the processes of computation	
• Adds, subtracts, multiplies, and divides whole numbers and decimals	76–84, 85–94, 95, 96–99, 100–105, 106
• Understands the properties of and the relationships among addition, subtraction, multiplication, and division	95, 96–99, 100–105, 106
• Adds and subtracts simple fractions	107–112
• Uses specific strategies (e.g., rounding) to estimate computations and to check the reasonableness of computational results	113–115
• Tells time to five minutes	126–127
Understands and applies basic and advanced properties of the concepts of measurement	
• Understands relationships between measures	116–120, 125
• Knows approximate size of basic standard units and relationships between them	121–122
• Selects and uses appropriate units of measurement, according to type and size of unit	123–124
Understands and applies basic and advanced properties of the concepts of geometry	
• Knows basic geometric language for describing and naming shapes	128–129

Social Studies Standards and Benchmarks	Page Numbers
History	
Understands the history of a local community and how communities in North America varied long ago	
• Knows geographical settings, economic activities, food, clothing, homes, crafts, and rituals of Native American societies long ago	130
• Understands the difficulties encountered by people in pioneer farming communities	131
• Knows the problems in past communities, the different perspectives of those involved, the choices people had, and the solutions they chose	132, 134

Meeting Standards *(cont.)*

Social Studies Standards and Benchmarks *(cont.)*	Page Numbers
History *(cont.)*	
Understands the people, events, problems, and ideas that were significant in creating the history of their state	
• Understands the nature, distribution, and migration of human populations on Earth's surface	136, 140
Understands how democratic values came to be, and how they have been exemplified by people, events, and symbols	
• Understands how people have helped make the community a better place to live	133–134
• Understands the basic ideas set forth in the Declaration of Independence and the U.S. Constitution, and the figures responsible for these documents	141–142
• Understands how songs, symbols, and slogans demonstrate freedom of expression and the role of protest in a democracy	143–145
• Knows the Pledge of Allegiance and patriotic songs, poems, and sayings that were written long ago, and understands their significance	144
• Understands the people, events, problems, and ideas that were significant in creating the history of their state	145
• Understands the basic principles of American democracy	146
• Understands how people over the last 200 years have continued to struggle to bring to all groups in American Society the liberties and equality promised in the basic principles of American democracy	147
• Understands the historical events and democratic values commemorated by major national holidays	148
Geography	
Understands the characteristics and uses of maps, globes, and other geographic tools and technologies	
• Knows the basic elements of maps and globes	137–139
Knows the location of places, geographic features, and patterns of the environment	
• Knows the approximate location of major continents, mountain ranges, and bodies of water on Earth	135, 138

Meeting Standards *(cont.)*

Science Standards and Benchmarks	Page Numbers
Understands atmospheric processes and the water cycle	
• Knows that water exists in the air in different forms and changes from one form to another through various processes	159
Understands Earth's composition and structure	
• Knows that fossils provide evidence about the plants and animals that lived long ago and the nature of the environment at that time	160
Understands the composition and structure of the universe and Earth's place in it	
• Knows that night and day are caused by Earth's rotation on its axis	161
• Knows that Earth is one of several planets that orbit the sun and that the moon orbits Earth	162–163
Understands the principles of heredity and related concepts	
• Knows that many characteristics of an organism are inherited from its parents, and other characteristics result from an individual's interactions with the environment	156
Understands relationships among organisms and their physical environment	
• Knows that the transfer of energy is essential to all living organisms	149
• Knows that changes in the environment can have different effects on different organisms	157
• Knows the organization of simple food chains and food webs	158
Understands the sources and properties of matter	
• Knows that matter has different states	150
• Knows that the mass of a material remains constant whether it is together, in parts, or in a different state	151
• Knows that matter has different states and that each state has distinct physical properties	150–152
Understands forces and motion	
• Knows the relationship between the strength of a force and its effect on an object	153–155
Understands the nature of scientific knowledge	
• Understands that models can be used to represent and predict changes in objects, events, and processes	164–165
Understands the nature of scientific inquiry	
• Knows that scientists use different kinds of investigations depending on the questions they are trying to answer	166–167

A is for Ant

Part 1

Directions: Trace each cursive letter. Then, write each letter at least five times.

a

a

a

a

Part 2

Directions: Trace each word. Then, write each word at least three times.

Ant

Ant

ant

ant

D is for Dog

Part 1

Directions: Trace each cursive letter. Then, write each letter at least five times.

D

D

d

d

Part 2

Directions: Trace each word. Then, write each word at least three times.

Dog

Dog

dog

dog

E is for Egg

Part 1

Directions: Trace each cursive letter. Then, write each letter at least five times.

$\mathcal{E}$

$\mathcal{E}$

e

e

Part 2

Directions: Trace each word. Then, write each word at least three times.

Egg

Egg

egg

egg

F is for Fairy

Part 1

Directions: Trace each cursive letter. Then, write each letter at least five times.

Part 2

Directions: Trace each word. Then, write each word at least two times.

G is for Goat

Part 1

Directions: Trace each cursive letter. Then, write each letter at least five times.

Part 2

Directions: Trace each word. Then, write each word at least three times.

H is for Home

Part 1

Directions: Trace each cursive letter. Then, write each letter at least five times.

_H_

_H_

_h_

_h_

Part 2

Directions: Trace each word. Then, write each word at least three times.

Home

Home

home

home

I is for Igloo

Part 1

Directions: Trace each cursive letter. Then, write each letter at least five times.

l

l

i

i

Part 2

Directions: Trace each word. Then, write each word at least two times.

Igloo

Igloo

igloo

igloo

J is for Jam

Part 1

Directions: Trace each cursive letter. Then, write each letter at least five times.

Part 2

Directions: Trace each word. Then, write each word at least three times.

K is for Key

Part I

Directions: Trace each cursive letter. Then, write each letter at least five times.

K

K

k

k

Part 2

Directions: Trace each word. Then, write each word at least three times.

Key

Key

key

key

L is for Lion

Part I

Directions: Trace each cursive letter. Then, write each letter at least five times.

_L_

_L_

_l_

_l_

Part 2

Directions: Trace each word. Then, write each word at least three times.

Lion

Lion

lion

lion

M is for Mice

Part I

Directions: Trace each cursive letter. Then, write each letter at least five times.

M

M

m

m

Part 2

Directions: Trace each word. Then, write each word at least three times.

Mice

Mice

mice

mice

N is for Nut

Part 1

Directions: Trace each cursive letter. Then, write each letter at least five times.

Part 2

Directions: Trace each word. Then, write each word at least three times.

O is for Ocean

Part 1

Directions: Trace each cursive letter. Then, write each letter at least five times.

O

O

o

o

Part 2

Directions: Trace each word. Then, write each word at least two times.

Ocean

Ocean

ocean

ocean

P is for Party

Part 1

Directions: Trace each cursive letter. Then, write each letter at least five times.

P

P

p

p

Part 2

Directions: Trace each word. Then, write each word at least two times.

Party

Party

party

party

Q is for Quilt

Part 1

Directions: Trace each cursive letter. Then, write each letter at least five times.

Q

Q

q

q

Part 2

Directions: Trace each word. Then, write each word at least two times.

Quilt

Quilt

quilt

quilt

R is for Rake

Part 1

Directions: Trace each cursive letter. Then, write each letter at least five times.

R

R

r

r

Part 2

Directions: Trace each word. Then, write each word at least three times.

Rake

Rake

rake

rake

S is for Snow

Part 1

Directions: Trace each cursive letter. Then, write each letter at least five times.

Part 2

Directions: Trace each word. Then, write each word at least two times.

T is for Tiger

Part 1

Directions: Trace each cursive letter. Then, write each letter at least five times.

T

T

t

t

Part 2

Directions: Trace each word. Then, write each word at least two times.

Tiger

Tiger

tiger

tiger

U is for Unit

Part 1

Directions: Trace each cursive letter. Then, write each letter at least five times.

U

U

u

u

Part 2

Directions: Trace each word. Then, write each word at least two times.

Unit

Unit

unit

unit

V is for Violin

Part 1

Directions: Trace each cursive letter. Then, write each letter at least five times.

$\mathcal{V}$

$\mathcal{V}$

v

v

Part 2

Directions: Trace each word. Then, write each word at least two times.

Violin

Violin

violin

violin

W is for Whale

Part 1

Directions: Trace each cursive letter. Then, write each letter at least five times.

W

W

w

w

Part 2

Directions: Trace each word. Then, write each word at least two times.

Whale

Whale

whale

whale

X is for X-ray

Part 1

Directions: Trace each cursive letter. Then, write each letter at least five times.

Part 2

Directions: Trace each word. Then, write each word at least two times.

Y is for Yellow

Part 1

Directions: Trace each cursive letter. Then, write each letter at least five times.

Y

Y

Y

Y

Part 2

Directions: Trace each word. Then, write each word at least two times.

Yellow

Yellow

yellow

yellow

Z is for Zipper

Part 1

Directions: Trace each cursive letter. Then, write each letter at least five times.

Z

Z

z

z

Part 2

Directions: Trace each word. Then, write each word at least two times.

Zipper

Zipper

zipper

zipper

Numbers

Part 1

Directions: Trace the number words. Then, write each word one time.

zero   *five*

one   *six*

two   *seven*

three   *eight*

four   *nine*

Part 2

Directions: Practice writing more number words in cursive on the spaces below. Find the answer for each problem, and write the answer on the line.

Example: Four plus four equals _____ *eight* _____.

1. One plus one equals _____.

2. Three plus three equals _____.

3. Five minus five equals _____.

4. Two plus two equals_____.

Putting It All Together

Directions: Read the following paragraph. Then, rewrite the paragraph on the lines provided using your best cursive writing. Continue on another sheet of paper, if needed.

Cats are wonderful pets. Cats are very friendly. They enjoy spending time with their caring owners. There are many different types of cats to choose from when picking out a cat for a pet. No matter what type of cat a person gets, he or she is getting a great pet and a loving companion for years to come.

What's Common and Proper?

Some nouns are common nouns, and some nouns are proper nouns.

A *common noun* is usually not capitalized (unless it is the first word of a sentence or in a title). A common noun is not specific. Some examples of common nouns are the words *boy* or *apple*.

A *proper noun* is always capitalized. A proper noun names a specific person, place, or thing. Some examples of proper nouns are *Gabe, Hawaii,* or *Thursday.*

Directions: Read each sentence. Draw a circle around each proper noun. Draw a rectangle around each common noun.

1. Monday is a holiday.

2. My friend Tammy is a very nice girl.

3. Bella decorated a cake.

4. Leo and Leiana are two beautiful kittens.

5. Helena read her book and then watched television.

6. Terrell ate pizza for supper.

7. Christmas and Hanukkah are in the month of December.

8. Sophie saw a monkey at the zoo.

9. Ben wished on a star.

10. The teacher asked Shannon to read the story.

11. Kelly watched the movie.

12. Tristan caught the mouse.

More Than One?

Nouns can be singular or plural. A *singular noun* names one person, place, thing, or idea. A *plural noun* names more than one person, place, thing, or idea.

Singular	Plural
dog	dogs
box	boxes
baby	babies
child	children

Part 1

Directions: Look at each picture. Write the singular noun that names each picture.

1. _____

2. _____

3. _____

4. _____

Part 2

Directions: Look at each picture. Write the plural noun that names each picture.

1. _____

2. _____

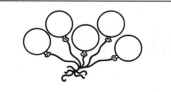

3. _____

4. _____

Simple Subjects Are Very Simple

The *simple subject* of a sentence is who or what the sentence is about.

> **Example:** Brandy gave the ball to Austin.

Who gave the ball to Austin? Brandy gave him the ball. Therefore, *Brandy* is the simple subject of the sentence. Brandy is who the sentence is about.

The simple subject is usually a noun, but sometimes it can be a pronoun. A *pronoun* is a word that takes the place of a noun. *I, we, you, he, she, it,* and *they* are all examples of pronouns that can be the subject.

> **Example:** She gave the ball to Austin.

Directions: Read each sentence. Find the simple subject. Write the simple subject on the line provided.

_____ 1. He climbed up the tree.

_____ 2. Katie sent the letter to her aunt.

_____ 3. The radio did not work.

_____ 4. The game started at noon.

_____ 5. My friend met me at the party.

_____ 6. They ate lunch with Ben.

_____ 7. Rabbits run fast.

_____ 8. I am happy today.

_____ 9. The family went on vacation.

_____ 10. Summer is a fun season.

Simple Predicates Can Be Simple

The *simple predicate* of the sentence is what the subject of the sentence is doing. The simple predicate (s.p.) can also be a word that links the subject to something else. The simple predicate is always a verb, but it can be either an **action verb** or a **linking** verb.

Examples

Carole <u>told</u> Rhonda a secret.   Carole <u>is</u> Rhonda's sister.
↑   ↑
action verb   **linking verb**

Directions: Complete the following sentences by writing a simple predicate on the line provided.

1. Jack _____ a cake in the new oven.

2. The boys _____ on the basketball team.

3. The puppy _____ the bone in the front yard.

4. Some people _____ to go on vacations.

5. The bird _____ above the trees.

6. She _____ movies with her family.

7. Cassie _____ the tennis match.

8. Kristen _____ a wonderful and exciting story.

9. Simon and Tessa _____ with their friends.

10. My mother _____ me with my homework.

Something Extra: Write a sentence of your own. Circle the simple predicate.

_____

Past, Present, and Future

Verbs have tense. This means a verb can happen in the present, in the past, or in the future.

Present	→	I <u>smile</u> when I'm happy.
Past	→	I <u>smiled</u> at the funny clown.
Future	→	I <u>will smile</u> when my chores are done!

Directions: Read each sentence. The verb is underlined for you. If the verb is present tense, write "present" on the line provided. If the verb is past tense, write "past" on the line provided. If the verb is future tense, write "future" on the line provided.

_____ 1. Our teacher <u>told</u> us a story.

_____ 2. She <u>tells</u> us to lower our voices when we're in the library.

_____ 3. He <u>saw</u> his favorite movie last week.

_____ 4. He <u>sees</u> a lot of movies.

_____ 5. He <u>will see</u> the new movie as soon as it comes out.

_____ 6. I <u>carry</u> packages to the car every day.

_____ 7. Tim <u>carried</u> the packages to the house.

_____ 8. Kim <u>will paint</u> the walls of her bedroom next Sunday.

_____ 9. I <u>laughed</u> when I heard his funny joke.

_____ 10. I <u>laugh</u> when my dog performs a trick.

Verbs and More Verbs

Directions: Below is a list of action verbs. Choose five of the verbs to help you complete the sentence starters that are given to you. Use one of the verbs plus your own words to finish each sentence. Use each verb only once.

Hint: If you need to, you can add endings such as *-ed, -ing, -s,* etc. to the verbs you use.

Action Verbs	hop	skip	walk	run
	listen	talk	sing	jump
	go	give	sit	laugh
	yell	tell	stop	move

1. At the birthday party, I _____

_____

2. The teacher told me _____

_____

3. Yesterday I _____

_____

4. When I get home from school, I _____

_____

5. I couldn't believe it when my friend _____

_____

Describing Words

An *adjective* is a word that describes a noun or a pronoun.

An adjective tells *how many, which one,* or *what kind* about the word it describes.

Examples

Twenty balloons	→	how many
This book	→	which one
Pretty girl	→	what kind

Directions: Write an adjective that helps complete each sentence. Read the new sentences.

1. The __________________ book was one of my favorite books in the library.
2. My __________________ friend invited me to spend the night.
3. Can you see the __________________ mouse?
4. He has __________________ baseball cards in his collection.
5. Her __________________ television show was on last night.
6. The __________________ boy played at the playground.
7. There were __________________ candles on the birthday cake.
8. At the zoo, there was a __________________ monkey.
9. I saw a __________________ bug outside in the grass.
10. My pet is the __________________ pet in the world!
11. __________________ girl sits next to me every day.
12. My __________________ cat is a great pet.

All Adverbs

Adverbs are words that describe verbs, adjectives, or other adverbs. Adverbs tell *how, when, where,* or *to what extent* about the words they describe.

Examples

He moved easily through the water.   (*Easily* tells how he moved.)

He went to the store yesterday.   (*Yesterday* tells when he went.)

He went there with his friend.   (*There* tells where he went.)

He ate too many chips.   (*Too* tells to what extent he ate.)

Part 1

Directions: Read each sentence. Draw a circle around each adverb.

1. My friend is very kind.

2. The turtle moved slowly but won the race.

3. Let's go to the movies tomorrow.

4. Please put your coat there.

5. He is so funny!

6. I never eat chocolate.

Part 2

Directions: In the space below, write two sentences. Use at least one adverb in each sentence. Circle each adverb.

1. _____

_____

2. _____

_____

Words that Connect

Conjunctions are words that connect. *For, and, nor, but, or, yet,* and *so* are all conjunctions.

Examples

I want pizza, salad, *and* fruit.

He wanted to go, *so* he finished all of his homework.

Part 1

Directions: Read each sentence. Write the conjunction from the parentheses that best completes each sentence.

1. Keith _____ (and, but) Robert play on the same football team.

2. Either Olivia _____ (yet, or) Katherine will sit beside Edward.

3. I want to go to school, _____ (so, but) I forgot to do my homework.

4. He is my friend, _____ (nor, yet) he still upsets me sometimes.

5. The teacher gave the class a party, _____ (for, yet) everyone did well on the test.

Part 2

Directions: Circle the conjunction in each sentence. Write the conjunction on the line.

1. Jack and Jill should not have gone up the hill._____

2. She went to the store, but she did not buy anything. _____

3. I want the chocolate ice cream or the mint ice cream._____

4. Neither Kim nor Kelly likes to play sports. _____

5. Corinne is a happy person, so she has many friends._____

Watch Those Double Negatives

Some words are negative words. *Not, never, no,* and *hardly* are all examples of words that are negative words. Two negative words should not be used together in the same sentence.

Examples

I can hardly reach that shelf.	→	Correct
I cannot hardly reach that shelf.	→	Incorrect

Directions: Look at each balloon. Use a green crayon to color the balloons that do not contain double negatives.

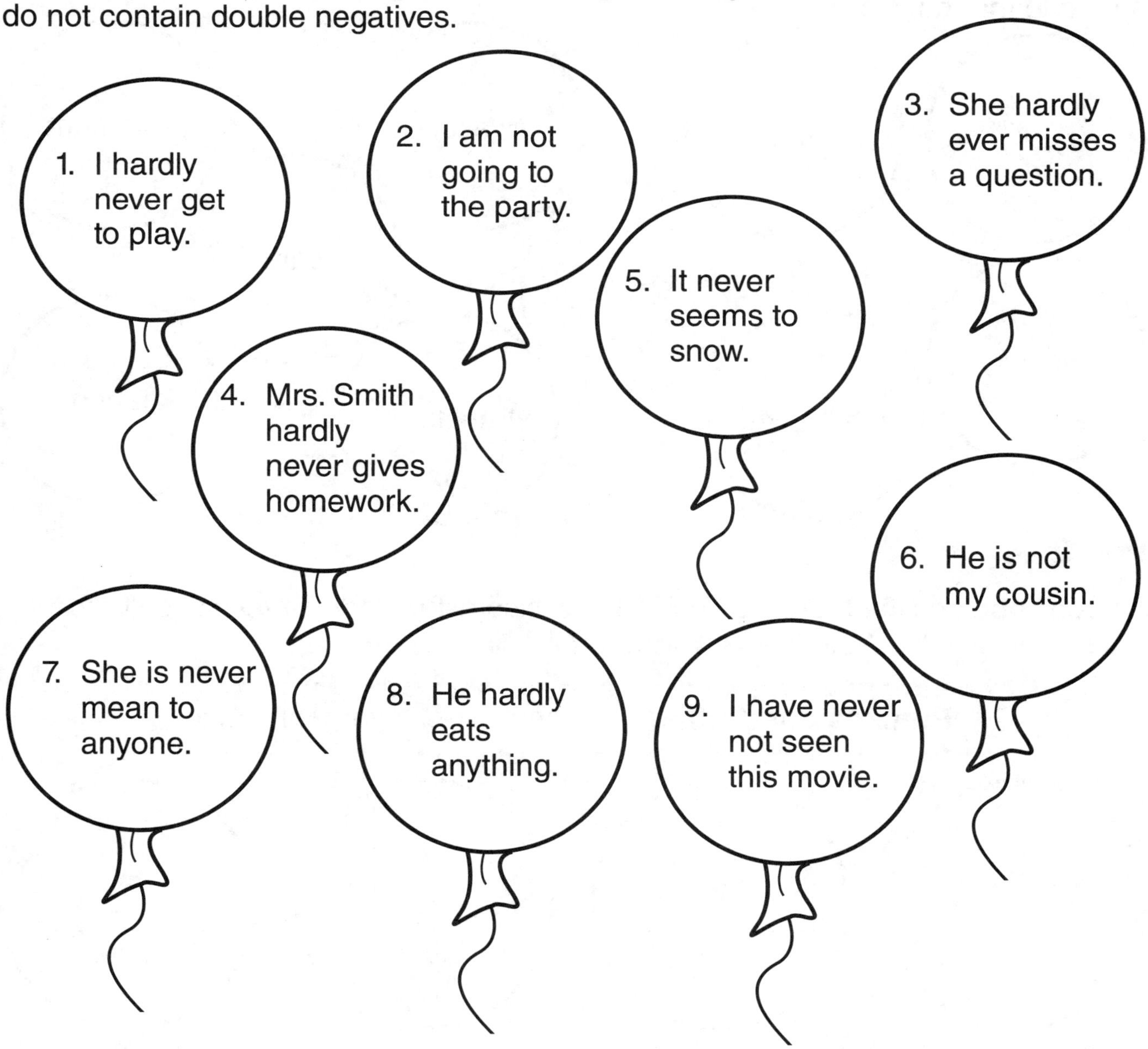
1. I hardly never get to play.
2. I am not going to the party.
3. She hardly ever misses a question.
4. Mrs. Smith hardly never gives homework.
5. It never seems to snow.
6. He is not my cousin.
7. She is never mean to anyone.
8. He hardly eats anything.
9. I have never not seen this movie.

Recognizing Prefixes and Suffixes

A *prefix* is added to the beginning of a word. A *suffix* is added to the end of a word. When added to root words, prefixes and suffixes help create new words.

> **Examples**
>
> Prefix ➡ <u>re</u> + appear = reappear
>
> Suffix ➡ friend + <u>ly</u> = friendly

Part 1

Directions: Color the circles that have words where a prefix or suffix has been added to the root word.

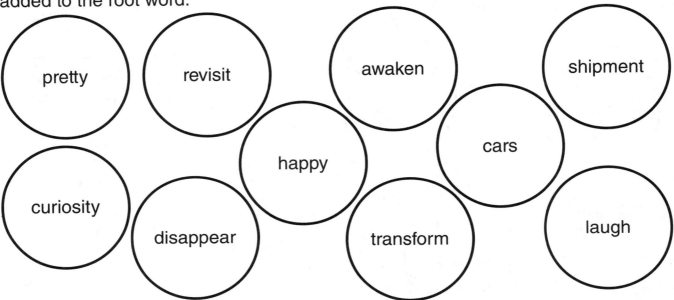

pretty

revisit

awaken

shipment

curiosity

happy

cars

disappear

transform

laugh

Part 2

Directions: Look at the words inside the circles below. Add a prefix or suffix to create new words. Write the new word on the line.

Prefixes and Suffixes	ment re over en mis

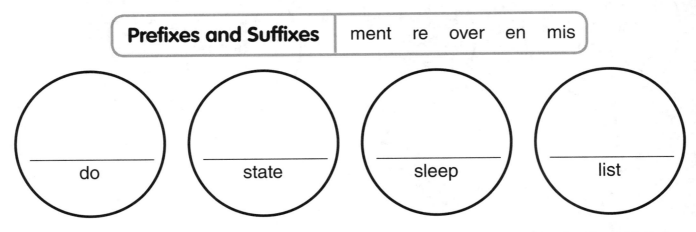

do

state

sleep

list

The Book of Words

A *dictionary* has words listed alphabetically. A dictionary will tell the reader many things about a word. One important thing a dictionary does is give the definition(s) for a word. A dictionary might also tell how many syllables are in a word or what part of speech the word is.

Part 1

Directions: Look at the list of words. Place them in alphabetical order as they would appear in a dictionary.

Word Bank
tent
shirt
horse
money
book
ant
summer
paper
cup
happy
boy
quiet

_____   _____

_____   _____

_____   _____

_____   _____

_____   _____

Part 2

Directions: Choose two of the words listed above, and write their dictionary definitions on the lines below.

1. _____

2. _____

Putting It All Together

Contractions are new words that are created out of two other words. Use an apostrophe (**'**) to help make the new word.

> **Examples**
>
> is + not = isn't
>
> she + is = she's

Directions: Choose from the list of contractions to help fill in the blanks.

Contractions	weren't	can't	didn't	don't	should've
	aren't	he's	it's	hasn't	she's

1. Mark _____ do his homework because he doesn't understand the problems.

2. I think _____ going to put his name on the list to try out for baseball.

3. Please _____ be so loud.

4. It _____ rained in four weeks.

5. Karen _____ cleaned up her room.

6. We _____ surprised when he won first place.

7. _____ going to be a great day.

8. I _____ tie my shoe.

9. _____ the prettiest girl I know.

10. They _____ coming to Riley's birthday party this weekend.

It's Proper to Capitalize

Proper nouns are words that are capitalized. A proper noun names a specific person, place, or thing and must start with a capital letter.

> **Examples**
>
> Mrs. Smith   →   person
>
> Louisville, Kentucky   →   place
>
> Washington Monument   →   thing

Directions: Read each sentence. Add a proper noun in the blank provided. Be sure to capitalize any proper noun that is used.

1. Mr. _____ gave me some spelling homework.

2. Yesterday we ate at _____, my favorite restaurant.

3. My birthday is in the month of _____.

4. Carla's favorite day of the week is _____.

5. _____ sits near me in class.

6. We went shopping at _____ , a store near my house, to buy some more school supplies.

7. Judy and _____ went to the movies last week.

8. Sadie can speak both English and _____.

9. _____ is the name of the city where I live.

10. On _____ , the day after Tuesday, she went to the dentist for her appointment.

Something Extra: Write a sentence of your own. Be sure to include at least two proper nouns. Circle the proper nouns you use.

_____

Capital Quotes

The words a person says are often placed inside quotation marks. The first letter of the first word inside the quotation marks is always capitalized.

> **Example:** Brett said, "Please pass the peas."

Directions: Draw three lines under the lowercase letter in each quote that should be capitalized. Write the capital letter above the corrected lowercase letter.

Example: Sue said, "N͟o I can't do it."

1. "our book reports are due on Monday," Jesse said.

2. Irene asked, "does anyone have any gum?"

3. Tessa said, "my dog is the cutest dog in the world."

4. "please pass the salt," Ken said.

5. Lucy cried, "i think my arm is broken!"

6. Austin said, "red is my favorite color."

7. "i wish I could go, too," Amanda said.

8. "when I turn ten, I'm getting my ears pierced," Kelly told her friend.

9. "do you want to play?" Edward asked.

10. Sandra said, "my doll's arm is broken."

11. Abbie asked, "can you come over to my house and play?"

12. "today is Thursday," the teacher said.

End It

There are three ending punctuation marks that can be used at the end of a sentence: the period (**.**), the question mark (**?**), and the exclamation point (**!**).

A *period* is used after a statement or a mild command.

I like you**.**   Go get my books**.**

A *question mark* is used after a question.

Do you like me**?**   Will you get my books**?**

An *exclamation point* is used to show strong emotion.

I think I love you**!** Go get my books, now**!**

Part 1

Directions: Read each sentence. Add the correct ending punctuation mark.

1. The house is on fire____   4. I like artichokes____

2. Do you know what time it is____   5. Look behind you____

3. My name is Linda____   6. Is he coming to school____

Part 2

Directions: Beside each number is an ending punctuation mark. Write a sentence that will end with the punctuation mark that is given.

1. (**?**) _____

2. (**.**) _____

3. (**!**) _____

How Does It End?

All sentences have ending punctuation. A sentence can end with one of three types of punctuation: a period (**.**), a question mark (**?**), or an exclamation point (**!**).

> Use a *period* if the sentence is a statement or a mild command.
>
> Use a *question mark* if the sentence asks a question.
>
> Use an *exclamation point* if the sentence shows strong emotion.

Directions: Look at each column. Choose a starter for your sentence and an ending for your sentence. Write the five new sentences on the lines provided. Be sure to add the correct ending punctuation.

Sentence Starters
How do you
I think I will
How beautiful
What are you
Will you please
My best friend is
I wish you would
We will eat supper

Sentence Endings
after I finish
start the game
be my friend
listen to me
go to the movies
the sunset looks
a very nice person
doing on Friday

1. _____

_____

2. _____

_____

3. _____

_____

4. _____

_____

5. _____

_____

This, This, and This

Commas are used to separate items listed in a series. If there are three or more items listed, use a comma to separate each one.

> **Example:** I went to Paris, Rome, and London.

Directions: Add commas as needed to the sentences below. If the sentence is correct as written, write the letter **C** on the line.

_____ 1. We ordered pizza spaghetti and lasagna.

_____ 2. My favorite sports are basketball soccer and swimming.

_____ 3. I wish I could have a dog a cat and a gerbil for my pets.

_____ 4. Please stop laughing and shouting during the movie.

_____ 5. For class I need paper a pencil and a book.

_____ 6. My best friends are Tristan and Hayden.

_____ 7. My favorite months are February March and April.

_____ 8. Mercury Venus and Earth are the planets that are closest to the sun.

_____ 9. We have music class on Monday Tuesday and Wednesday.

_____ 10. We need to get milk bread and cheese from the grocery store.

Something Extra: Write a sentence of your own listing three things. Be sure to write in commas wherever they are needed.

_____

_____

Commas in Dates and Addresses

A *comma* is used when writing the date. A comma should be placed between the day of the month and the year.

> **Examples:** February 19, 2011   July 4, 1776

A *comma* is also used when writing an address. A comma should be placed between the street address and the city and between the city and the state.

> **Example:** I live at 210 Oak Drive, Happy Haven, Missouri.

Directions: Write a complete sentence that will answer each question. Use commas in each answer.

Example: What is your school's address? <u>My school's address is</u> <u>2103 Happy Highway, Anytown, Tennessee 34567.</u>

1. When is your birthday? _____

   _____

2. What is today's date? _____

   _____

3. What is your home address? _____

   _____

4. What are three things you like to eat? _____

   _____

5. Who are three people you know? _____

   _____

6. What three numbers come after the number three? _____

   _____

Exact Words

Quotation marks go around a person's exact words. Do not put quotation marks around words the person did not say.

> **Example:** "I like to ride my bike," Tim said.

Quotation marks are not around the words *Tim said* because Tim only said, "I like to ride my bike."

Directions: Read each sentence. Add quotation marks where they are needed.

1. I wish I had three wishes, Allison said.

2. What would you do with three wishes? Kristen asked.

3. First, I would wish for a lot of toys, Allison said.

4. What would you wish for next? Kristen asked.

5. I would wish for some toys for you, too, Allison replied.

6. That is so nice! Kristen exclaimed.

7. I can be nice, Allison said.

8. What would you wish for with your final wish? Kristen asked.

9. Oh, that's easy, Allison said.

10. Then, Allison added, I would wish that you would want to give all of your new toys to me!

Something Extra: What do you think Kristen would say about Allison's third and final wish? Write what Kristen would say on the lines below. Remember to use quotation marks around Kristen's exact words.

Kristen said, _____

_____

Someone's Speaking

Quotation marks are used around words to show when someone is speaking. Quotation marks only go around what someone is saying or the person's exact words.

> **Examples**
>
> "I am in sixth grade, Chris said." → Incorrect
>
> "I am in sixth grade," Chris said. → Correct

Directions: Read each sentence. Add quotation marks where they are needed. If the sentence is correct, write a **C** on the line provided.

_____ 1. Jeff said, "Friday is my favorite day of the week."

_____ 2. Do you know what time it is? Thomas asked.

_____ 3. My dog chased my cat up a tree, Kelly said.

_____ 4. Would you pass the ketchup, please? Cara asked.

_____ 5. Alicia said, "You are a good friend."

_____ 6. Go get me a milkshake, Jake demanded.

_____ 7. "Look at that cowboy," Anna said.

_____ 8. Chloe said, I wish today was my birthday.

_____ 9. "What time did you get here?" Mark asked.

_____ 10. Amanda said, I can't come to your party.

Time and Colons

A *colon* (:) is used to separate time. A colon is placed between the hour and the minutes when writing down time.

> **Examples**
>
> 7:30 AM
>
> 2:15 in the afternoon
>
> 4:00 PM

Part 1

Directions: Read each sentence. Add a colon wherever it is needed.

1. I need to go to lunch at 12 00 noon.

2. My bedtime is 8 30 in the evening.

3. I have to catch the school bus at 6 30 in the morning.

4. Can you tell me when it is 5 00 PM?

Part 2

Directions: Answer each question with a complete sentence. Use a colon in each answer.

1. What time do you eat lunch?

   _____

2. What time do you get home from school?

   _____

3. What time do you usually eat dinner?

   _____

4. What time do you get up on Saturday?

   _____

Being Friendly

Below is a friendly letter. The letter has ten capitalization or punctuation mistakes.

Directions

1. Correct each capitalization mistake by placing three small lines under the lowercase letter that should be capitalized. These marks are called editing marks. Write the capitalized letter above the corrected lowercase one.

Example: M J
mrs. joost

2. Correct each punctuation mistake by adding in the correct punctuation.

1090 Elm Street

Anytown kansas 43718

August 26 2010

Dear Ella

    How are you I am doing well. I miss seeing you each day like we did at camp. Camp was really a lot of fun

    Please write to me over the school year I will write you back. I am going to make a scrapbook using all of our pictures. I will send you copies of the photos

                        Your friend

                        linda

Alike and Different

Words that are *synonyms* are words that are the same or alike.

> **Example:** *pretty* and *beautiful*

Words that are *antonyms* are words that are opposite or different.

> **Example:** *pretty* and *ugly*

Part 1

Directions: Read each word. Circle the letter of the word choice that is a *synonym* for the given word.

1. nice   **a.** kind   **b.** mean

2. little   **a.** small   **b.** large

3. small   **a.** tiny   **b.** huge

4. mean   **a.** nice   **b.** unkind

5. sad   **a.** happy   **b.** upset

Part 2

Directions: Read each word. Write down a word that is an *antonym* for the listed word.

1. cute   _____

2. nervous   _____

3. hungry   _____

4. sleepy   _____

5. short   _____

Same Sound, Different Spelling

Some words sound alike but are spelled differently and have different meanings. These words are called *homophones.*

Directions: Choose the correct homophone for each sentence. Circle the correct answer.

1. That is (there, their) house.

2. Please give me (they're, their) phone number.

3. (Its, It's) a long story.

4. She is (too, two) young to get her ears pierced.

5. (Their, They're) going to be late to the movies.

6. Tell him (two, to) call me on my cell phone.

7. He is (too, to) short to reach the top shelf.

8. Have you met (they're, their) older brother?

9. She is (two, too) years younger than I am.

Something Extra: Use the words *two, they're,* and *it's* in sentences you create.

1. _____

    _____

2. _____

    _____

3. _____

    _____

Why Write It?

When authors write, they write for a reason. Maybe they want to entertain their audience, or maybe they want to inform or give their audience information.

Directions: Look at each picture below. Circle the letter of the correct reason why each one might have been written.

1. Encyclopedia **a.** to give information **b.** to entertain	**2.** How to Recycle **a.** to persuade or convince **b.** to entertain
3. EXAMINER Five Department Battles Blaze **a.** to entertain **b.** to give information	**4.** Healthy Cooking **a.** to give information **b.** to entertain
5. Once upon a time... **a.** to entertain **b.** to persuade or convince	**6.** Caring for Birds **a.** to persuade or convince **b.** to give information

Something Extra: On the back of this page, draw a picture of a book in your classroom. When you are finished with your picture, write the reason why you think the author wrote this book.

A Problem and a Solution

Plot is the series of events in a story or the main problem that happens in a story. How the problem is solved is also part of the plot, but it has a special name. This part of the plot is called the *resolution.*

> In the story of the three little pigs, the problem is that a wolf is trying to eat the pigs. The pigs solve the problem by moving into a house the wolf cannot blow down and then catching the wolf as he comes down the chimney.

Directions: Plot is all about finding a solution for a problem. Read each problem below. Write how you would resolve each problem. Be sure to write in complete sentences.

1. **Problem:** You want an ice-cream cone. The cost is $1.00. You only have 50¢. What will you do?

   Resolution: _____

   _____

2. **Problem:** You want to get a dog for a pet. Your parents do not want to get a dog because your yard is very small. What can you do?

   Resolution: _____

   _____

3. **Problem:** You have a test today. You forgot to study. Your test is in one hour. What will you do?

   Resolution: _____

   _____

4. **Problem:** You borrowed your friend's book. You spilled a glass of milk on the book. What can you do?

   Resolution: _____

   _____

First This, Then That

If people don't brush their teeth, they will probably get cavities. This is an example of *cause and effect*. The *cause* is not brushing, and the *effect* of not brushing is getting cavities.

Directions: Read each effect. Circle the letter of the correct cause.

1. **Effect:** The twins learned to ride horses.

   Cause: **a.** The twins took piano lessons.

   b. The twins took horseback-riding lessons.

2. **Effect:** The third grader made the honor roll.

   Cause: **a.** The third grader studied and worked hard.

   b. The third grader missed a lot of school.

3. **Effect:** The boy was very sleepy.

   Cause: **a.** The boy stayed up too late.

   b. The boy ate a good breakfast.

4. **Effect:** The girl got a sunburn.

   Cause: **a.** She fell asleep in the sun.

   b. She ate too many donuts.

5. **Effect:** The boy caught a fish.

   Cause: **a.** The boy stayed inside all day.

   b. The boy went fishing.

6. **Effect:** The little girl had a birthday party.

   Cause: **a.** The girl had a birthday.

   b. The girl went to sleep.

7. **Effect:** The little boy was sick.

   Cause: **a.** The boy read a book.

   b. The boy's best friend had a cold.

8. **Effect:** The baby got a bottle.

   Cause: **a.** The baby was crying.

   b. The baby was taking a bath.

When and Where

The *setting* of a story tells *when* and *where* the story happens.

Directions: Think about the things that have happened in your life. Tell about the setting that goes with each event listed below.

1. **A past birthday party**

    a. When did it happen? _____

    b. Where did it happen? _____

2. **A fun trip**

    a. When did it happen? _____

    b. Where did it happen? _____

3. **A time you were sick**

    a. When did it happen? _____

    b. Where did it happen? _____

4. **A special day**

    a. When did it happen? _____

    b. Where did it happen? _____

5. **A fun time with friends**

    a. When did it happen? _____

    b. Where did it happen? _____

Telling the Story

Every story has a *point of view,* or someone who is telling the story.

A story written in the **1st person** uses the words *I* or *me.*

   <u>I</u> drink a glass of milk every day.

A story written in the **2nd person** uses the word *you.*

   <u>You</u> are finishing your homework.

A story written in the **3rd person** uses the words *he, she, it,* or *they.* It can also name specific people, such as *Mom, Brett,* and *Lindsey.*

   <u>She</u> was tired after swimming all day.

Directions: Read each short description. Write down what "person" is being named in the story: 1st person, 2nd person, or 3rd person.

1. Mrs. Brody told the class to get their papers ready for the quiz. She saw that everyone was ready except for two children. She was not happy.

   What "person" is named in the story? _____

2. Every time I get on an airplane, I feel nervous. I am worried that we are going to have a rough landing. Luckily, we have always had safe and steady landings. I am grateful to fly on planes that have such excellent airline pilots.

   What "person" is named in the story? _____

3. The stuffed animal you got for your birthday is adorable. You must be so happy with your new lion! Did you tell your parents how much you love it?

   What "person" is named in the story? _____

4. The ringmaster announced that the circus was about to begin. He told the audience to look at the center ring. He said that the lions would appear in just a few moments.

   What "person" is named in the story? _____

5. My mother told me to clean up my room. After my room is clean, she promised me that we would go out and get some ice cream.

   What "person" is named in the story? _____

Metaphors and Similes

Metaphors and *similes* are types of figurative language that are used to compare things that are not alike.

> If you want to say your brother is very messy, you might say that your brother is a pig. By comparing your brother to a pig, you give a better picture of how messy he truly is. He is not an actual pig. You are simply making that comparison. This is an example of a metaphor.
>
> A *metaphor* makes a comparison between two unlike things. A *simile* also makes a comparison between two unlike things, but a simile uses the words *like* or *as* to make the comparison.
>
> **Simile** → My brother is *as messy as* a pig.   **Metaphor** → My brother is a pig.

Directions: Read each sentence. Decide if a metaphor or a simile is being used. Then, circle the letter of the correct answer.

1. My youngest sister is an angel.

    a. metaphor   **b.** simile

2. My oldest sister is as mean as a snake.

    a. metaphor   **b.** simile

3. The wind is like a roaring lion.

    a. metaphor   **b.** simile

4. The movie star's eyes sparkle like diamonds.

    a. metaphor   **b.** simile

5. The librarian is as quiet as a mouse.

    a. metaphor   **b.** simile

6. My grandfather is a wise, old owl.

    a. metaphor   **b.** simile

7. The baby is as sweet as candy.

    a. metaphor   **b.** simile

8. My mom was boiling mad over my bad grade.

    a. metaphor   **b.** simile

A Big, Fun Word

One type of figurative language is *onomatopoeia.* Onomatopoeia is a big word, but its meaning is simple. Onomatopoeia is a word for a noise—it is a word that sounds like what it is. We know a bee makes a noise as it flies by, but how do you write down the sound a bee makes? The word "buzz" is used for the noise a bee makes. The word "buzz" is an example of onomatopoeia.

Directions: Animal sounds like "oink" are common onomatopoeia. Look at the picture of each animal. Write a word for the sound each animal makes.

Fun with the Same Sound

Alliteration is figurative language that is fun for your tongue! Alliteration is the repetition of the same consonant sound at the beginning of a group of words.

Please put the papers in the purple pail. This is an example of alliteration. Notice the "p" sound is repeated at the beginning of several of the words. Tongue twisters have alliteration in them.

Directions: Read each example of alliteration below. Add at least two words anywhere in the sentence to help continue the sound.

Hint: It's okay to add a few extra words that do not have the same consonant sound, but you must add some words that do continue the same consonant sound.

> **Example**
> She sells shoes.
> <u>She sells silver shoes to Sally and Sandy.</u>

1. Tom told the truth.

   _____

2. Randy reads regularly.

   _____

3. Carla can't quit.

   _____

4. Mom makes meatloaf.

   _____

5. Dan's dog digs.

   _____

6. Fran has five freckles.

   _____

Show What You Know

Directions: Identify each figurative language element that is used. Write the correct answer on the line provided.

> alliteration   metaphor   onomatopoeia   simile

_____ 1. She is as kind as an angel.

_____ 2. "Meow, meow," purred the hungry cat.

_____ 3. Stop stepping in the sand.

_____ 4. Carole and Carla ate chocolate cake.

_____ 5. The wind is like a warrior.

_____ 6. He is such a clown.

_____ 7. The dogs said, "Woof, woof!'

_____ 8. "Oink, oink," went the pigs.

_____ 9. Pass the peas, please.

_____ 10. He is a snake.

Something Extra: Choose one of the figurative language elements listed above. Write your own example below. See if a classmate can guess what type of figurative language you have written.

_____

_____

Categories of Literature

Think about the types of foods you eat. Food can be divided into different categories. There are fruits, vegetables, meats, grains, etc. They are all foods, but they are all different types of food.

Writing can also be divided into categories. There are fairy tales, folktales, myths, poetry, historical fiction, biographies, autobiographies, and many, many more types. In writing, these categories are called *genres.*

Directions: Look at each genre. Circle the letter of the story title that fits each one.

1. **fairy tale**

   a. *The Three Little Pigs*

   b. *Easy Cooking Ideas*

2. **autobiography**

   a. *My Life*

   b. *How to Care for Your New Pet*

3. **poetry**

   a. *Building Your Own Dog House*

   b. *Fly High in the Sky*

4. **historical fiction**

   a. *Abraham Lincoln at the Fair*

   b. *The Magical Dragon*

5. **myth**

   a. *How to Be a Better Student*

   b. *Cupid's Lost Arrow*

6. **folktale**

   a. *Cowboy Carl Captures the Wind*

   b. *Funny Jokes and Riddles*

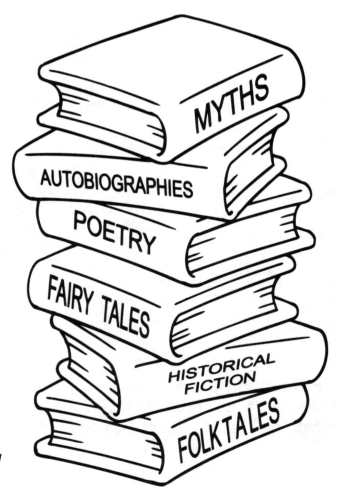

All in the View

Writing is divided into categories called *genres*. There are many different types of genres such as fairy tales, myths, poetry, folktales, nonfiction, historical fiction, biographies, autobiographies, and more. Each type of writing has characteristics or things about it that make it unique.

Directions: Look at each picture. Circle the letter of the genre that is shown.

1.

a. fairy tale   **b.** historical fiction

3.

a. myth   **b.** biography

2.

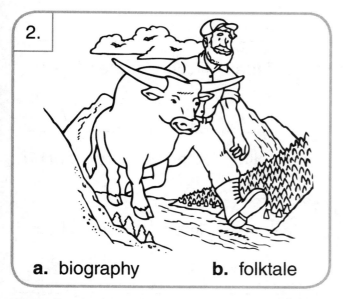

a. biography   **b.** folktale

4.

a. fairy tale   **b.** myth

Something Extra: If you wrote a story about your life, what type of genre would your story be? Write your response on the back of this page, and draw a picture to go with your choice of genre.

Knowing the Parts

Most textbooks have special sections or parts. Three important parts of some school books are the *table of contents,* the *index,* and the *glossary.*

> The *table of contents* is at the front of the book. It tells what information is inside the book. And it usually tells the page number that the information starts on.
>
> The *index* is at the back of the book. It has an alphabetical list of information in the book. It tells what page number you can find the information on.
>
> The *glossary* is also at the back of the book. It is a dictionary of important words found inside the book.

Directions: Answer each question by choosing from the words below.

> table of contents   glossary   index

1. In a science book, where could you find out what chapter will have information about the solar system?

   _____

2. Where in a social studies book would you find the definition for the word *pioneer*?

   _____

3. In a math book, where would you find the definition for the word *subtraction*?

   _____

4. Where in a school book would you find definitions for important words from the chapter?

   _____

5. If you wanted to find out what page in a science book has information about Earth, where would you look?

   _____

Using a Glossary

A *glossary* is a special type of dictionary. It is in the back of a textbook or other informational book. The glossary will have words and definitions that are found in the book.

Directions: Below is a list of words that might be found in the glossary of a science book. Write definitions for the words to complete the glossary.
Hint: If you need help, use a dictionary or glossary of your own.

Word	Definition
1. carnivore	_____
	_____
2. Earth	_____
	_____
3. fossil	_____
	_____
4. gravity	_____
	_____
5. herbivore	_____
	_____
6. omnivore	_____
	_____
7. planet	_____
	_____
8. star	_____
	_____

Say It in a Few Words

When you summarize, you do not retell something word for word. You tell only the most important parts. If you read a good book and wanted to tell someone about it, you would summarize or sum it up. You wouldn't tell someone everything about the book.

Directions: Practice summarizing by answering the questions below. Use complete sentences.

1. What did you do yesterday?

   _____

   _____

2. What happened today at school?

   _____

   _____

3. Write about a time you were really happy.

   _____

   _____

4. Write about a time you got something you really wanted.

   _____

   _____

5. What are you planning to do this weekend?

   _____

   _____

Are They Odd or Even?

Even numbers can be divided into two sets that have the same number in each.
Odd numbers cannot be divided evenly.

Directions: Look at each set of things below. Decide if they are *odd* or *even*.
Write the answer on the line below the set.

1. _even_

2. _even_

3. _even_

4. _odd_

5. _odd_

6. _even_

7. _odd_

8. _odd_

The Key to Addition

Being careful when you add is one key to addition!

Directions: Add to find the sum.

1.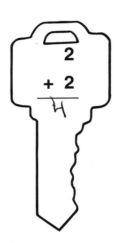
$$\begin{array}{r} 2 \\ +\ 2 \\ \hline 4 \end{array}$$

2.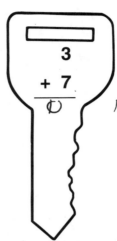
$$\begin{array}{r} 3 \\ +\ 7 \\ \hline 0 \end{array}$$

3.
$$\begin{array}{r} 2 \\ +\ 4 \\ \hline 6 \end{array}$$

4.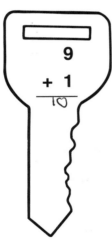
$$\begin{array}{r} 9 \\ +\ 1 \\ \hline 10 \end{array}$$

5.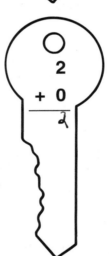
$$\begin{array}{r} 2 \\ +\ 0 \\ \hline 2 \end{array}$$

6.
$$\begin{array}{r} 3 \\ +\ 4 \\ \hline 7 \end{array}$$

7.
$$\begin{array}{r} 5 \\ +\ 4 \\ \hline 9 \end{array}$$

8.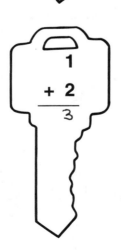
$$\begin{array}{r} 1 \\ +\ 2 \\ \hline 3 \end{array}$$

9.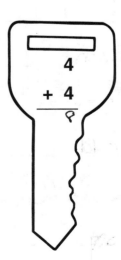
$$\begin{array}{r} 4 \\ +\ 4 \\ \hline 8 \end{array}$$

Reverse Addition

Reversing or flipping the order in which you add numbers in a simple addition problem does not change the sum or answer.

Example

1 + 5 = 6

5 + 1 = 6

Think about it: If someone gave you one dollar, and then someone gave you five dollars, how much money would you have? If you said six dollars, then you are right! Now, what if that same person offered you five dollars, and then he offered you one dollar to go with the five dollars. How much money is he giving you? That's right! You would have six dollars again. Reversing the order of the numbers in the equation does not make a difference when you are adding.

Directions: Look at each addition problem. Add to find the answer.

1. 2 + 4 = _____ 4 + 2 = _____	6. 8 + 9 = _____ 9 + 8 = _____
2. 3 + 7 = _____ 7 + 3 = _____	7. 5 + 3 = _____ 3 + 5 = _____
3. 6 + 5 = _____ 5 + 6 = _____	8. 6 + 7 = _____ 7 + 6 = _____
4. 1 + 8 = _____ 8 + 1 = _____	9. 1 + 3 = _____ 3 + 1 = _____
5. 9 + 3 = _____ 3 + 9 = _____	10. 5 + 9 = _____ 9 + 5 = _____

The Heart of Addition

Directions: Add the two-digit numbers to find each sum.

1.
$$12 + 10$$

2.
$$14 + 14$$

3.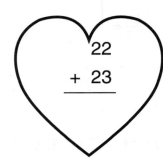
$$22 + 23$$

4.
$$18 + 13$$

5.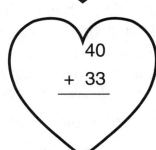
$$40 + 33$$

6.
$$55 + 30$$

7.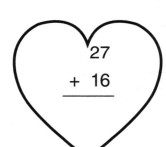
$$27 + 16$$

8.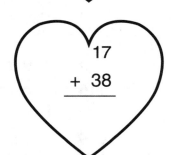
$$17 + 38$$

9.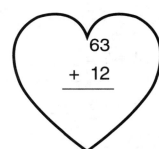
$$63 + 12$$

10.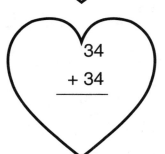
$$34 + 34$$

11.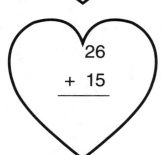
$$26 + 15$$

12.
$$19 + 16$$

13.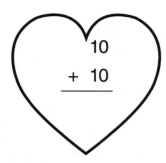
$$10 + 10$$

14.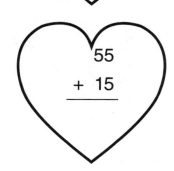
$$55 + 15$$

15.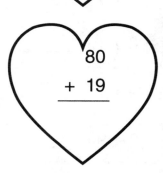
$$80 + 19$$

"Tri" This

Directions: Add the three-digit numbers to find each sum.

1.
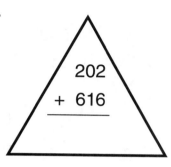

$$\begin{array}{r} 202 \\ +\ 616 \\ \hline \end{array}$$

2.
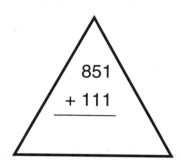

$$\begin{array}{r} 851 \\ +\ 111 \\ \hline \end{array}$$

3.

$$\begin{array}{r} 333 \\ +\ 432 \\ \hline \end{array}$$

4.
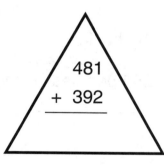

$$\begin{array}{r} 771 \\ +\ 100 \\ \hline \end{array}$$

5.
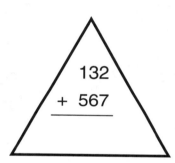

$$\begin{array}{r} 132 \\ +\ 567 \\ \hline \end{array}$$

6.
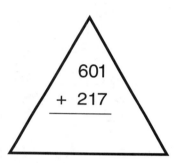

$$\begin{array}{r} 601 \\ +\ 217 \\ \hline \end{array}$$

7.
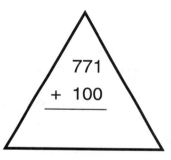

$$\begin{array}{r} 481 \\ +\ 392 \\ \hline \end{array}$$

8.

$$\begin{array}{r} 521 \\ +\ 401 \\ \hline \end{array}$$

9.

$$\begin{array}{r} 118 \\ +\ 722 \\ \hline \end{array}$$

10.
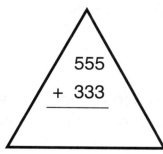

$$\begin{array}{r} 555 \\ +\ 333 \\ \hline \end{array}$$

11.
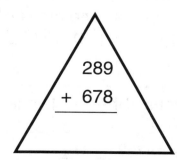

$$\begin{array}{r} 289 \\ +\ 678 \\ \hline \end{array}$$

12.
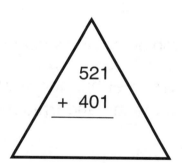
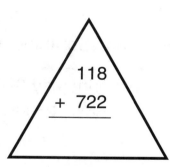
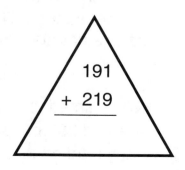

$$\begin{array}{r} 191 \\ +\ 219 \\ \hline \end{array}$$

Expert at Addition

Part 1

Directions: Add the numbers to find the answers.

1. 310 + 202	2. 403 + 304	3. 775 + 114	4. 543 + 412
5. 413 + 505	6. 289 + 700	7. 333 + 222	8. 189 + 471
9. 761 + 161	10. 678 + 256	11. 800 + 112	12. 617 + 393

Part 2

Directions: Solve the word problems. Show your work on the back.

1.	Katherine had 600 pennies. Her brother Braden had 253 pennies. How many total pennies did Katherine and Braden have? _____
2.	333 students were going to the pep rally. 123 students were visiting from another school. These students were also going to the pep rally. How many students were going to the pep rally? _____
3.	Kelly wanted to recycle cans. She had two large trash bags filled with cans. She had 388 cans in one bag. She had 398 cans in the other bag. How many total cans did Kelly have? _____

The Decimal Place

Some numbers have decimals. When you add numbers that have decimals, the decimal stays in the same place.

Example	17.20
	+ 22.12
	39.32

Directions: Find each sum. Remember to keep the decimal in the same place when writing your answer.

1.	2.	3.	4.
22.18 + 17.12	11.33 + 88.12	46.46 + 26.26	13.21 + 16.15
5.	**6.**	**7.**	**8.**
6.8 + 9.2	18.42 + 20.11	3.2 + 2.3	51.21 + 15.15
9.	**10.**	**11.**	**12.**
8.12 + 1.11	7.1 + 1.7	67.09 + 20.21	71.09 + 20.10
13.	**14.**	**15.**	**16.**
9.77 + 1.02	34.12 + 13.23	7.2 + 1.7	22.22 + 33.33

Decimal Magic

When you are adding numbers that have decimals, do not move the decimals. They just magically stay where they are!

Example	11.12
	+ 13.21
	24.33

Directions: Add each problem. Be sure to include the decimal.

1.　　22.23
　　+ 11.31
　　─────

2.　　18.67
　　+ 10.51
　　─────

3.　　87.10
　　+ 10.01
　　─────

4.　　72.22
　　+ 22.22
　　─────

5.　　32.66
　　+ 22.33
　　─────

6.　　17.11
　　+ 11.17
　　─────

7.　　19.17
　　+ 62.01
　　─────

8.　　25.18
　　+ 44.23
　　─────

9.　　12.02
　　+ 12.12
　　─────

10.　　63.19
　　+ 37.20
　　─────

11.　　9.2
　　+ 2.3
　　─────

12.　　17.98
　　+ 33.87
　　─────

13.　　43.21
　　+ 17.32
　　─────

14.　　12.76
　　+ 67.21
　　─────

Read It and Write

Directions: Solve each word problem. Show your work.

1. Dallas has $5.23 in her piggy bank. She needs $4.72 more to be able to buy the toy she wants. What is the total cost of the toy Dallas wants to buy?	**Answer:** _____
2. Missy has 25 stuffed animals. Her big sister Katie has 43 stuffed animals. Her little sister Cassandra has 29 stuffed animals. How many stuffed animals do the sisters have altogether?	**Answer:** _____
3. Kelly was having fun at the egg hunt. She had already found 73 eggs. Fifteen minutes later she found 27 more eggs. She won the hunt because she had more eggs than anyone else. How many eggs did Kelly have at the end of the hunt?	**Answer:** _____
4. There are 20 students in Mrs. Gilbreath's third grade class. Mrs. Myles has 19 students in her third grade class. Miss Connolly has 22 students in her third grade class. How many total students are there in the teachers' classes?	**Answer:** _____
5. Tim has a stamp collection. He has 75 stamps in his collection. His sister Hannah has 35 stamps in her collection. How many total stamps do Tim and Hannah have?	**Answer:** _____

Word Problems Rock!

Directions: Read and then solve each addition word problem. Be sure and show your work in the space provided.

1. Susan loves music. She has eight songs she listens to over and over again. Her mother also loves music. She has five favorite songs that she likes to listen to. How many total favorite songs do Susan and her mother listen to?

   Answer:

   _____

   Show your work:

2. Terrell saw a band perform in the park. The band had five members. Terrell noticed the band did not have anyone playing the keyboard. After the band was finished playing, Terrell asked if he could join the band. Once Terrell joined as the keyboard player, how many members were in the band?

   Answer:

   _____

   Show your work:

3. There are thirty-six black keys on a piano. There are fifty-two white keys on a piano. How many total keys are on a piano?

   Answer:

   _____

   Show your work:

4. Mrs. Angie has ten piano students. There are three new students who want to join Mrs. Angie's class. If Mrs. Angie lets the three new students join, how many total students will Mrs. Angie have?

   Answer:

   _____

   Show your work:

Simply Picture This

Directions: Subtract to find the answers.

1.
$$\begin{array}{r} 6 \\ -\ 3 \\ \hline \end{array}$$

2.
$$\begin{array}{r} 9 \\ -\ 5 \\ \hline \end{array}$$

3.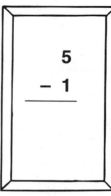
$$\begin{array}{r} 5 \\ -\ 1 \\ \hline \end{array}$$

4.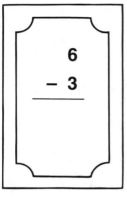
$$\begin{array}{r} 3 \\ -\ 2 \\ \hline \end{array}$$

5.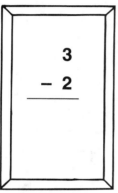
$$\begin{array}{r} 8 \\ -\ 2 \\ \hline \end{array}$$

6.
$$\begin{array}{r} 7 \\ -\ 5 \\ \hline \end{array}$$

7.
$$\begin{array}{r} 4 \\ -\ 2 \\ \hline \end{array}$$

8.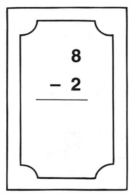
$$\begin{array}{r} 9 \\ -\ 2 \\ \hline \end{array}$$

9.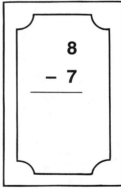
$$\begin{array}{r} 8 \\ -\ 7 \\ \hline \end{array}$$

10.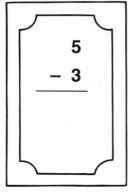
$$\begin{array}{r} 5 \\ -\ 3 \\ \hline \end{array}$$

11.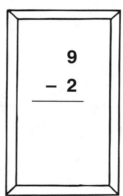
$$\begin{array}{r} 6 \\ -\ 4 \\ \hline \end{array}$$

12.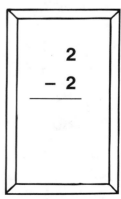
$$\begin{array}{r} 2 \\ -\ 2 \\ \hline \end{array}$$

Subtracting Double Digits

Directions: Subtract to find each difference.

1.   15
    − 13
	2. 54
	    − 12
		3. 72
		    − 12
			4. 35
			    − 25

5.   20
    − 10
	6. 63
	    − 33
		7. 95
		    − 73
			8. 45
			    − 11

9.   48
    − 37
	10. 78
	    − 24
		11. 69
		    − 14
			12. 18
			    − 14

13.   82
    − 32
	14. 88
	    − 17
		15. 12
		    − 11
			16. 98
			    − 52

17.   99
    − 88
	18. 50
	    − 20
		19. 41
		    − 21
			20. 15
			    − 11

Race into Action with Double-Digit Subtraction

Part 1

Directions: Subtract to find the answer.

1.
```
  55
− 22
────
```

2.
```
  18
− 13
────
```

3.
```
  78
− 23
────
```

4.
```
  12
− 11
────
```

5.
```
  69
− 18
────
```

6.
```
  28
− 17
────
```

7.
```
  41
− 11
────
```

8.
```
  19
− 18
────
```

9.
```
  51
− 30
────
```

10.
```
  95
− 82
────
```

Part 2

Directions: Solve each word problem.

1. Cade has 53¢. He spends 22¢ on bubble gum. How much money does Cade have left after he buys the bubble gum?

   Answer: _____

2. Abby has thirty-five pages in her book that she needs to read. She read twelve pages, but then she had to go to bed. How many pages does Abby still need to read?

   Answer: _____

Regroup When You Subtract

Sometimes when you subtract, you need to "borrow" from another number. This is also called *regrouping*.

Example	$\begin{array}{r} \overset{6\ 1}{\cancel{7}2} \\ -\ 63 \\ \hline 9 \end{array}$

Directions: Subtract to find each difference. Regroup whenever needed.

1. $\begin{array}{r} 25 \\ -\ 18 \\ \hline \end{array}$
2. $\begin{array}{r} 87 \\ -\ 42 \\ \hline \end{array}$
3. $\begin{array}{r} 97 \\ -\ 49 \\ \hline \end{array}$
4. $\begin{array}{r} 12 \\ -\ 10 \\ \hline \end{array}$

5. $\begin{array}{r} 76 \\ -\ 55 \\ \hline \end{array}$
6. $\begin{array}{r} 48 \\ -\ 39 \\ \hline \end{array}$
7. $\begin{array}{r} 93 \\ -\ 88 \\ \hline \end{array}$
8. $\begin{array}{r} 54 \\ -\ 18 \\ \hline \end{array}$

9. $\begin{array}{r} 46 \\ -\ 17 \\ \hline \end{array}$
10. $\begin{array}{r} 68 \\ -\ 12 \\ \hline \end{array}$
11. $\begin{array}{r} 70 \\ -\ 33 \\ \hline \end{array}$
12. $\begin{array}{r} 59 \\ -\ 49 \\ \hline \end{array}$

13. $\begin{array}{r} 22 \\ -\ 13 \\ \hline \end{array}$
14. $\begin{array}{r} 67 \\ -\ 59 \\ \hline \end{array}$
15. $\begin{array}{r} 15 \\ -\ 13 \\ \hline \end{array}$
16. $\begin{array}{r} 77 \\ -\ 44 \\ \hline \end{array}$

Three Times the Fun

Subtracting a lot of numbers creates a lot of subtraction fun.

Directions: Use subtraction to solve each problem. Borrow whenever needed.

1.	376 − 218	2.	874 − 289	3.	777 − 490	4.	901 − 521
5.	341 − 216	6.	318 − 278	7.	489 − 398	8.	621 − 128
9.	821 − 221	10.	321 − 300	11.	765 − 321	12.	452 − 430
13.	567 − 532	14.	612 − 513	15.	121 − 117	16.	822 − 129
17.	698 − 567	18.	371 − 365	19.	431 − 123	20.	771 − 176

Triple-Decker Subtraction

Directions: Use subtraction to solve each problem.

1.　　761
　　− 234

2.　　341
　　− 231

3.　　632
　　− 521

4.　　976
　　− 210

5.　　451
　　− 333

6.　　871
　　− 231

7.　　656
　　− 412

8.　　702
　　− 602

9.　　590
　　− 319

10.　　445
　　− 210

11.　　998
　　− 109

12.　　689
　　− 378

13.　　278
　　− 201

14.　　562
　　− 532

15.　　745
　　− 689

16.　　201
　　− 112

17.　　298
　　− 189

18.　　677
　　− 456

Hop Into Some Subtraction Review

Directions: Use subtraction to solve each problem.

1. 772
   − 658

2. 18
   − 12

3. 89
   − 43

4. 982
   − 761

5. 541
   − 234

6. 412
   − 321

7. 67
   − 41

8. 91
   − 32

9. 21
   − 16

10. 651
    − 578

11. 87
    − 36

12. 14
    − 10

13. 321
    − 123

14. 43
    − 23

Decimals: One Simple Rule

Subtracting with decimals is easy as long as you remember one simple rule: Do not move the decimal.

Example
$$\begin{array}{r} 7.7 \\ -\ 2.1 \\ \hline 5.6 \end{array}$$

Notice the decimal's placement did not change.

Directions: Practice subtracting with decimals. Solve the subtraction problems below. Remember not to move the decimals.

1. $\begin{array}{r} 8.1 \\ -\ 3.8 \\ \hline \end{array}$ 2. $\begin{array}{r} 9.3 \\ -\ 7.1 \\ \hline \end{array}$ 3. $\begin{array}{r} 22.1 \\ -\ 12.1 \\ \hline \end{array}$ 4. $\begin{array}{r} 76.2 \\ -\ 32.1 \\ \hline \end{array}$

5. $\begin{array}{r} 7.7 \\ -\ 6.6 \\ \hline \end{array}$ 6. $\begin{array}{r} 18.6 \\ -\ 13.2 \\ \hline \end{array}$ 7. $\begin{array}{r} 4.2 \\ -\ 2.1 \\ \hline \end{array}$ 8. $\begin{array}{r} 56.4 \\ -\ 34.3 \\ \hline \end{array}$

9. $\begin{array}{r} 2.9 \\ -\ 1.8 \\ \hline \end{array}$ 10. $\begin{array}{r} 82.9 \\ -\ 34.7 \\ \hline \end{array}$ 11. $\begin{array}{r} 6.7 \\ -\ 3.2 \\ \hline \end{array}$ 12. $\begin{array}{r} 11.11 \\ -\ 10.10 \\ \hline \end{array}$

Subtraction with Decimals

When subtracting with decimals, the decimal does not change places.

Example	765.98
	− 23.72
	742.26

Directions: Solve the subtraction problems below. Remember not to move the decimals.

1.	543.21 − 231.14	2.	467.18 − 451.19	3.	761.12 − 332.12	4.	123.67 − 101.23

5.	412.53 − 298.12	6.	978.11 − 732.14	7.	512.87 − 419.98	8.	674.23 − 312.43

9.	471.88 − 198.76	10.	698.12 − 444.12	11.	773.21 − 673.21	12.	396.78 − 227.07

13.	566.33 − 501.22	14.	178.91 − 123.02	15.	249.21 − 187.12	16.	502.29 − 401.19

Animal Subtraction

Directions: Read and solve each word problem. Be sure to show how you got your answer.

1. Mr. Johnson had 89 fish in his tank. His son, Wally, needed some fish for his new fish tank. Mr. Johnson gave Wally 33 fish for Wally's tank. After Mr. Johnson gave his son some fish, how many fish did Mr. Johnson have in his fish tank?

   Answer:
   _____

   Show your work:

2. Melissa went to the zoo. She had never been to the zoo before. One of her favorite places in the zoo was the butterfly house. The zoo worker told Melissa there were 300 butterflies. However, he also told Melissa some of the butterflies were being sent to a different zoo, so they could have a butterfly house. The zoo was giving away 140 butterflies. How many butterflies would be left once 140 were given away?

   Answer:
   _____

   Show your work:

3. Thomas had $357.89 in his savings account. He wanted to buy a pet parrot for his room. The parrot would be very expensive. Plus, he needed all of the supplies that would go with the new parrot. When the pet store rang up Thomas's bill, the total was $157.23. How much money did Thomas have left in his savings account once he paid for the parrot and all of the supplies?

   Answer:
   _____

   Show your work:

All Mixed Up

Directions: Solve each problem.

Hint: Be sure to check if the problem is an addition problem or a subtraction problem because the problems are all mixed up!

1. $\begin{array}{r} 23 \\ + 17 \\ \hline \end{array}$	2. $\begin{array}{r} 19 \\ - 13 \\ \hline \end{array}$	3. $\begin{array}{r} 47 \\ - 33 \\ \hline \end{array}$	4. $\begin{array}{r} 56 \\ + 45 \\ \hline \end{array}$
5. $\begin{array}{r} 43 \\ - 31 \\ \hline \end{array}$	6. $\begin{array}{r} 78 \\ - 52 \\ \hline \end{array}$	7. $\begin{array}{r} 98 \\ - 35 \\ \hline \end{array}$	8. $\begin{array}{r} 53 \\ + 22 \\ \hline \end{array}$
9. $\begin{array}{r} 46 \\ + 18 \\ \hline \end{array}$	10. $\begin{array}{r} 29 \\ - 23 \\ \hline \end{array}$	11. $\begin{array}{r} 89 \\ - 44 \\ \hline \end{array}$	12. $\begin{array}{r} 17 \\ + 18 \\ \hline \end{array}$
13. $\begin{array}{r} 64 \\ + 13 \\ \hline \end{array}$	14. $\begin{array}{r} 84 \\ - 32 \\ \hline \end{array}$	15. $\begin{array}{r} 22 \\ + 43 \\ \hline \end{array}$	16. $\begin{array}{r} 72 \\ - 41 \\ \hline \end{array}$
17. $\begin{array}{r} 85 \\ + 12 \\ \hline \end{array}$	18. $\begin{array}{r} 65 \\ - 39 \\ \hline \end{array}$	19. $\begin{array}{r} 19 \\ - 17 \\ \hline \end{array}$	20. $\begin{array}{r} 67 \\ + 16 \\ \hline \end{array}$

Multiplication and Addition Have Much in Common

Directions: Complete each pair of number sentences.

1. $2 + 2 + 2 =$ _____ $2 \times 3 =$ _6_

2. $4 + 4 =$ _____ $4 \times 2 =$ _8_

3. $3 + 3 + 3 + 3 + 3 =$ _____ $3 \times 5 =$ _15_

4. $1 + 1 + 1 + 1 + 1 + 1 =$ _____ $1 \times 6 =$ _6_

5. $8 + 8 + 8 + 8 + 8 =$ _____ $8 \times 5 =$ _40_

6. $7 + 7 + 7 =$ _____ $7 \times 3 =$ _21_

7. $9 + 9 + 9 + 9 + 9 + 9 + 9 =$ _____ $9 \times 7 =$ _63_

8. $5 + 5 + 5 + 5 =$ _____ $5 \times 4 =$ _20_

9. $6 + 6 + 6 + 6 + 6 + 6 + 6 =$ _____ $6 \times 7 =$ _41_

10. $2 + 2 + 2 + 2 =$ _____ $2 \times 4 =$ _8_

11. $8 + 8 =$ _____ $8 \times 2 =$ _16_

12. $9 + 9 + 9 =$ _____ $9 \times 3 =$ _27_

13. $10 + 10 + 10 + 10 =$ _____ $10 \times 4 =$ _40_

14. $11 + 11 + 11 =$ _____ $11 \times 3 =$ _33_

Fly High! Let's Multiply!

Directions: Multiply to find each product.

1.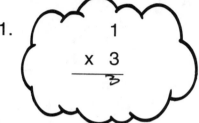
$$\begin{array}{r} 1 \\ \times\ 3 \\ \hline 3 \end{array}$$

2.
$$\begin{array}{r} 3 \\ \times\ 7 \\ \hline 21 \end{array}$$

3.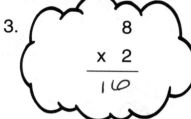
$$\begin{array}{r} 8 \\ \times\ 2 \\ \hline 16 \end{array}$$

4.
$$\begin{array}{r} 5 \\ \times\ 5 \\ \hline 29 \end{array}$$

5.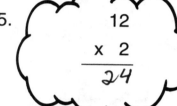
$$\begin{array}{r} 12 \\ \times\ 2 \\ \hline 24 \end{array}$$

6.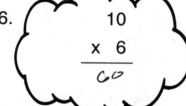
$$\begin{array}{r} 10 \\ \times\ 6 \\ \hline 60 \end{array}$$

7.
$$\begin{array}{r} 4 \\ \times\ 8 \\ \hline 32 \end{array}$$

8.
$$\begin{array}{r} 6 \\ \times\ 7 \\ \hline 41 \end{array}$$

9.
$$\begin{array}{r} 9 \\ \times\ 8 \\ \hline 72 \end{array}$$

10.
$$\begin{array}{r} 6 \\ \times\ 1 \\ \hline 6 \end{array}$$

11.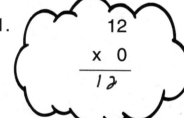
$$\begin{array}{r} 12 \\ \times\ 0 \\ \hline 12 \end{array}$$

12.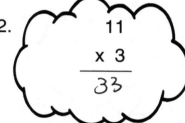
$$\begin{array}{r} 11 \\ \times\ 3 \\ \hline 33 \end{array}$$

13.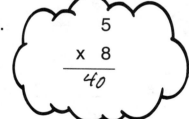
$$\begin{array}{r} 5 \\ \times\ 8 \\ \hline 40 \end{array}$$

14.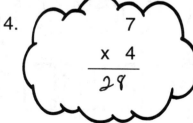
$$\begin{array}{r} 7 \\ \times\ 4 \\ \hline 28 \end{array}$$

Multiply Some More

Directions: Count the number of items in each group. Write the number on the first line. Then, multiply by the factor given to find the final product.

Example: ⬡ ⬡ ⬡   __3__ x 5 = __15__

1. ◯ ◯ ◯ ◯   ___ x 4 = _____

2. ☺ ☺ ☺ ☺ ☺   ___ x 6 = _____

3. ☆ ☆ ☆ ☆ ☆ ☆ ☆   ___ x 3 = _____

4. ☐ ☐ ☐   ___ x 8 = _____

5. △ △   ___ x 9 = _____

6. ♡ ♡ ♡ ♡ ♡ ♡   ___ x 7 = _____

7. ◇ ◇ ◇ ◇ ◇ ◇ ◇   ___ x 2 = _____

8. ◯ ◯ ◯ ◯ ◯ ◯ ◯ ◯ ◯ ◯   ___ x 4 = _____

9. ☐ ☐ ☐ ☐ ☐ ☐ ☐ ☐ ☐   ___ x 7 = _____

10. ☹ ☹ ☹ ☹ ☹ ☹ ☹   ___ x 4 = _____

Multiplying Dots Is Not Hard!

Directions: Count the number of dots on the back of each bug. Write the number on the first line. Complete the multiplication problem to find each product.

1.  _____ x 5 = _____	6. _____ x 7 = _____
2.  _____ x 8 = _____	7. _____ x 3 = _____
3.  _____ x 4 = _____	8. _____ x 11 = _____
4.  _____ x 10 = _____	9. _____ x 5 = _____
5.  _____ x 6 = _____	10.  _____ x 8 = _____

Making Connections

Solve the problems in each row. Do you see the connection between multiplying and dividing?

Directions: Complete each problem below.

1. 15 ÷ 3 = ___5___   3 x 5 = _____

2. 21 ÷ 7 = ___3___   7 x 3 = _____

3. 44 ÷ 4 = ___11___   4 x 11 = _____

4. 50 ÷ 10 = ___5___   10 x 5 = _____

5. 12 ÷ 3 = ___4___   3 x 4 = _____

6. 8 ÷ 2 = ___4___   2 x 4 = _____

7. 10 ÷ 5 = ___2___   5 x 2 = _____

8. 36 ÷ 4 = ___9___   4 x 9 = _____

9. 72 ÷ 9 = ___8___   9 x 8 = _____

10. 18 ÷ 3 = ___6___   3 x 6 = _____

11. 20 ÷ 4 = ___5___   4 x 5 = _____

12. 28 ÷ 7 = ___4___   7 x 4 = _____

13. 56 ÷ 8 = _____   8 x 7 = _____

14. 30 ÷ 3 = _____   3 x 10 = _____

15. 6 ÷ 2 = _____   2 x 3 = _____

16. 35 ÷ 7 = _____   7 x 5 = _____

17. 4 ÷ 2 = _____   2 x 2 = _____

18. 70 ÷ 7 = _____   7 x 10 = _____

Practice Division

Everyone knows that practice makes perfect. Use the problems below to practice your division skills and become . . . nearly perfect!

Directions: Find the answer to each division problem.

1. 24 ÷ 2 = _____

2. 36 ÷ 3 = _____

3. 24 ÷ 12 = _____

4. 25 ÷ 5 = _____

5. 16 ÷ 8 = _____

6. 55 ÷ 11 = _____

7. 21 ÷ 3 = _____

8. 10 ÷ 2 = _____

9. 36 ÷ 4 = _____

10. 77 ÷ 11 = _____

11. 42 ÷ 6 = _____

12. 49 ÷ 7 = _____

13. 81 ÷ 9 = _____

14. 80 ÷ 10 = _____

15. 48 ÷ 6 = _____

16. 12 ÷ 2 = _____

The Purr-fect Answer

Directions: Solve each division problem. Circle the letter of the correct answer.

1. $18 \div 2 = $ _____
   - **a.** 9
   - **b.** 3
   - **c.** 2

2. $28 \div 7 = $ _____
   - **a.** 3
   - **b.** 4
   - **c.** 7

3. $81 \div 9 = $ _____
   - **a.** 8
   - **b.** 6
   - **c.** 9

4. $144 \div 12 = $ _____
   - **a.** 11
   - **b.** 10
   - **c.** 12

5. $56 \div 8 = $ _____
   - **a.** 8
   - **b.** 7
   - **c.** 6

6. $121 \div 11 = $ _____
   - **a.** 8
   - **b.** 11
   - **c.** 3

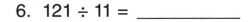

7. $10 \div 2 = $ _____
   - **a.** 3
   - **b.** 2
   - **c.** 5

8. $60 \div 12 = $ _____
   - **a.** 5
   - **b.** 10
   - **c.** 6

9. $36 \div 3 = $ _____
   - **a.** 8
   - **b.** 6
   - **c.** 12

10. $48 \div 4 = $ _____
    - **a.** 12
    - **b.** 4
    - **c.** 8

When Some Remains

When you divide one number into another, the problem may not always work out evenly. When this happens, the division problem will have a remainder.

Example

$$8\overline{\smash{)}29} \quad \begin{array}{r} 3\,\text{R}5 \\ \hline 29 \\ -24 \\ \hline 5 \end{array}$$

Directions: Divide each problem. Be sure to show all of your work.
Hint: Each problem will have a remainder.

1. $2\overline{\smash{)}79}$

2. $10\overline{\smash{)}87}$

3. $2\overline{\smash{)}11}$

4. $8\overline{\smash{)}81}$

5. $8\overline{\smash{)}97}$

6. $2\overline{\smash{)}7}$

7. $4\overline{\smash{)}99}$

8. $5\overline{\smash{)}22}$

9. $5\overline{\smash{)}68}$

10. $9\overline{\smash{)}22}$

11. $4\overline{\smash{)}55}$

12. $8\overline{\smash{)}18}$

13. $2\overline{\smash{)}13}$

14. $8\overline{\smash{)}92}$

15. $5\overline{\smash{)}17}$

16. $5\overline{\smash{)}48}$

Leftovers

See what's cooking below with division!

Directions: Complete each division problem. Remember that some problems might have something "left over." In division this is called the *remainder.*

1.

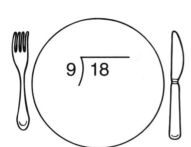

2.

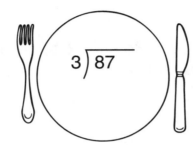

3.

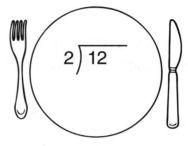

4.

5.

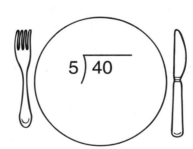

6.

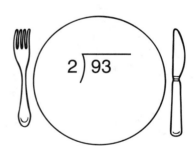

7.

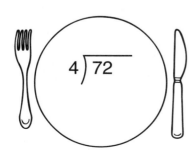

8.

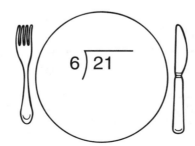

9.

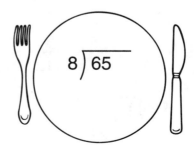

Divide and Conquer

Directions: Read the following word problems. Use division to find the correct answers.

1. Linda loves chocolate candy. She has 81 pieces of candy. She wants to divide her candy evenly among nine people. How many pieces of candy will each person get once Linda divides the candy?

   Answer:

   _____

   Show your work:

2. Thatcher has 100 baseball cards. He wants to divide the cards equally between his friend Keenan and himself. How many cards will each boy get if the cards are divided equally?

   Answer:

   _____

   Show your work:

3. Mrs. Ryder has 24 students in her class. She has 72 pencils to give to her 24 students. Mrs. Ryder wants each student to get the same number of pencils when she hands them out to the class. How many pencils will each student get?

   Answer:

   _____

   Show your work:

4. Thomas has 33 toy cars. His friends, Jim and Sam, have come over to his house to play. Thomas wants to divide his toy cars up evenly so that all three boys have the same number of cars. How many cars will each boy get?

   Answer:

   _____

   Show your work:

Mixed Practice

Directions: Below are multiplication and division problems. Solve each problem.

1. 5 x 10 = _____

2. 6 x 7 = _____

3. 18 ÷ 2 = _____

4. 9 x 2 = _____

5. 12 ÷ 6 = _____

6. 22 ÷ 11 = _____

7. 72 ÷ 9 = _____

8. 2 x 3 = _____

9. 1 x 10 = _____

10. 10 ÷ 2 = _____

11. 56 ÷ 7 = _____

12. 8 x 8 = _____

13. 44 ÷ 11 = _____

14. 10 x 9 = _____

15. 81 ÷ 9 = _____

16. 32 ÷ 8 = _____

17. 6 ÷ 3 = _____

18. 21 ÷ 7 = _____

19. 12 x 12 = _____

20. 10 x 11 =_____

Not the Whole Thing

A *fraction* is part of the whole thing. Think about the last time you had some cake, pie, or even pizza. Chances are, unless you were very, very hungry, you probably did not eat the entire cake, pie, or pizza. You probably ate only a slice or two. You ate a fraction or a part of the delicious food.

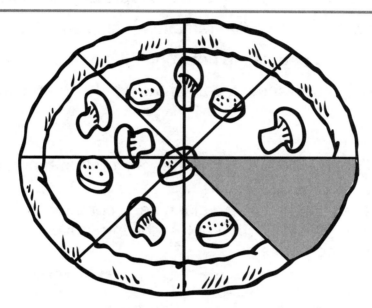

In this example, $\frac{1}{8}$ of the pizza is gone. There were eight total slices. One slice is gone, so $\frac{1}{8}$ is the fraction that is missing. The fraction that is left is $\frac{7}{8}$.

Directions: Study the shaded parts of each shape. Then, circle the letter of the answer choice that shows the correct fraction.

1. 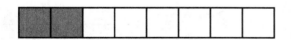   **a.** $\frac{6}{8}$ **b.** $\frac{2}{8}$ **c.** $\frac{2}{7}$

2. 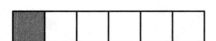   **a.** $\frac{1}{6}$ **b.** $\frac{5}{6}$ **c.** $\frac{2}{6}$

3.    **a.** $\frac{1}{3}$ **b.** $\frac{2}{3}$ **c.** $\frac{3}{3}$

Just a Part

A *fraction* is a part of something. A fraction is used to show a part of the whole.

> If there are eight people at your lunch table, and three of the eight people have lunch boxes, you can say $\frac{3}{8}$ of the people at your table brought their lunches to school. If the five remaining people had to buy lunch, you can also say $\frac{5}{8}$ of the people did not bring their lunch to school. The fractions $\frac{3}{8}$ and $\frac{5}{8}$ each show a part of the whole group that sits at your lunch table.

Directions: Read each problem. Write the fraction that represents each group.

1.	Seven of the ten children in the class have completed their homework. What fraction of the children have their homework complete? **Answer:** _____
2.	Amanda has one out of the five math problems on her math sheet completed. Shown as a fraction, how many math problems has Amanda already finished? **Answer:** _____
3.	Jackson had ten grapes. He has eaten three of the ten grapes. What fraction of the grapes has Jackson already eaten? **Answer:** _____
4.	Nine of the ten children in Mrs. Bailey's study group have turned in their book reports. What fraction of the children have turned in their reports to Mrs. Bailey? **Answer:** _____
5.	Olivia had five pieces of gum. She chewed two pieces. Shown as a fraction, how many pieces of gum did Olivia chew? **Answer:** _____

Looking at Fractions

Directions: Look at each group of pictures, and write a fraction for the answer.

1. What fraction of the children is smiling? _____

2. What fraction of the dogs has collars? _____

3. What fraction of the pencils needs to be sharpened? _____

4. What fraction of the cookies has a piece missing? _____

5. What fraction of the bugs has spots? _____

6. What fraction of the flowers has missing petals? _____

Adding Fractions

A fraction has two parts. The top number of a fraction is called the *numerator*. This represents the number of parts being looked at. The bottom number of a fraction is called the *denominator*. This represents the total number of parts in the whole. It is easy to add fractions when the denominator is the same.

When you add fractions with the same denominator, only the numerator changes. Does this sound confusing? Really, it's not. Just look at the example below:

> ➡ numerator
> ――――――――
> ➡ denominator $\dfrac{1}{4} + \dfrac{2}{4} = \dfrac{3}{4}$

Notice that the top numbers change, but the bottom number stays the same.

Directions: Add the following fractions. The first one has been done for you.

1. $\dfrac{2}{9} + \dfrac{6}{9} = \dfrac{8}{9}$

2. $\dfrac{1}{5} + \dfrac{2}{5} = $ ――――

3. $\dfrac{8}{12} + \dfrac{2}{12} = $ ――――

4. $\dfrac{1}{3} + \dfrac{2}{3} = $ ――――

5. $\dfrac{6}{8} + \dfrac{1}{8} = $ ――――

6. $\dfrac{1}{4} + \dfrac{1}{4} = $ ――――

7. $\dfrac{1}{3} + \dfrac{1}{3} = $ ――――

8. $\dfrac{4}{10} + \dfrac{5}{10} = $ ――――

9. $\dfrac{1}{4} + \dfrac{2}{4} = $ ――――

10. $\dfrac{2}{12} + \dfrac{4}{12} = $ ――――

11. $\dfrac{2}{5} + \dfrac{2}{5} = $ ――――

12. $\dfrac{1}{7} + \dfrac{2}{7} = $ ――――

13. $\dfrac{3}{9} + \dfrac{4}{9} = $ ――――

14. $\dfrac{5}{12} + \dfrac{6}{12} = $ ――――

15. $\dfrac{2}{5} + \dfrac{2}{5} = $ ――――

16. $\dfrac{1}{6} + \dfrac{3}{6} = $ ――――

Subtracting with Fractions

When the bottom numbers of fractions are the same number, you can easily subtract the fractions. The bottom number of a fraction is called the *denominator.* The top number is called the *numerator.*

$$\dfrac{\text{numerator}}{\text{denominator}} \qquad \dfrac{7}{8} - \dfrac{2}{8} = \dfrac{5}{8} \qquad \leftarrow \dfrac{\text{changes}}{\text{stays the same}} \leftarrow$$

Notice that the bottom number, the denominator, stays the same.

Directions: Subtract the following fractions. The first one has been done for you.

1. $\dfrac{4}{5} - \dfrac{3}{5} = \dfrac{1}{5}$

2. $\dfrac{3}{9} - \dfrac{2}{9} = $ _____

3. $\dfrac{5}{7} - \dfrac{2}{7} = $ _____

4. $\dfrac{2}{4} - \dfrac{1}{4} = $ _____

5. $\dfrac{6}{8} - \dfrac{3}{8} = $ _____

6. $\dfrac{2}{3} - \dfrac{1}{3} = $ _____

7. $\dfrac{8}{10} - \dfrac{5}{10} = $ _____

8. $\dfrac{11}{12} - \dfrac{9}{12} = $ _____

9. $\dfrac{4}{5} - \dfrac{2}{5} = $ _____

10. $\dfrac{6}{9} - \dfrac{2}{9} = $ _____

11. $\dfrac{4}{8} - \dfrac{3}{8} = $ _____

12. $\dfrac{9}{11} - \dfrac{5}{11} = $ _____

13. $\dfrac{7}{10} - \dfrac{2}{10} = $ _____

14. $\dfrac{3}{4} - \dfrac{2}{4} = $ _____

15. $\dfrac{4}{10} - \dfrac{3}{10} = $ _____

16. $\dfrac{5}{8} - \dfrac{1}{8} = $ _____

Fractions: Adding and Subtracting

Directions: Look over the problems below. If the problem is an addition problem, draw an oval around the problem. If the problem is a subtraction problem, do not draw anything. Then, add or subtract the fractions. The first one has been done for you.

1. $\dfrac{1}{4} + \dfrac{2}{4} = \dfrac{3}{4}$

2. $\dfrac{1}{9} + \dfrac{1}{9} =$ _____

3. $\dfrac{7}{8} - \dfrac{3}{8} =$ _____

4. $\dfrac{1}{5} + \dfrac{3}{5} =$ _____

5. $\dfrac{8}{9} - \dfrac{3}{9} =$ _____

6. $\dfrac{2}{4} - \dfrac{1}{4} =$ _____

7. $\dfrac{5}{12} + \dfrac{6}{12} =$ _____

8. $\dfrac{7}{11} - \dfrac{6}{11} =$ _____

9. $\dfrac{2}{6} + \dfrac{2}{6} =$ _____

10. $\dfrac{7}{12} + \dfrac{2}{12} =$ _____

11. $\dfrac{3}{4} - \dfrac{1}{4} =$ _____

12. $\dfrac{4}{5} - \dfrac{2}{5} =$ _____

13. $\dfrac{1}{3} + \dfrac{1}{3} =$ _____

14. $\dfrac{6}{8} - \dfrac{3}{8} =$ _____

15. $\dfrac{5}{10} + \dfrac{2}{10} =$ _____

16. $\dfrac{1}{6} + \dfrac{3}{6} =$ _____

17. $\dfrac{9}{12} - \dfrac{6}{12} =$ _____

18. $\dfrac{2}{7} + \dfrac{4}{7} =$ _____

Up or Down

Directions: Round each number to the nearest ten. Write the answer on the line provided.

> **Not Rounded:** 743
>
> **Rounded:** 740

If you round the number up, color in the arrow pointing up. If you round the number down, color in the arrow pointing down.

1. 321 _____ ⬆ ⬇   11. 234 _____ ⬆ ⬇

2. 678 _____ ⬆ ⬇   12. 856 _____ ⬆ ⬇

3. 812 _____ ⬆ ⬇   13. 513 _____ ⬆ ⬇

4. 123 _____ ⬆ ⬇   14. 746 _____ ⬆ ⬇

5. 175 _____ ⬆ ⬇   15. 356 _____ ⬆ ⬇

6. 561 _____ ⬆ ⬇   16. 612 _____ ⬆ ⬇

7. 423 _____ ⬆ ⬇   17. 622 _____ ⬆ ⬇

8. 279 _____ ⬆ ⬇   18. 708 _____ ⬆ ⬇

9. 487 _____ ⬆ ⬇   19. 487 _____ ⬆ ⬇

10. 534 _____ ⬆ ⬇   20. 333 _____ ⬆ ⬇

Rounding Rocks!

Directions: Round the following numbers to the nearest hundred. Circle the letter of the correct answer choice.

Examples: 732	782
a. (700) **b.** 800	**a.** 700 **b.** (800)

1. 123	2. 789	3. 567
a. 100	**a.** 800	**a.** 500
b. 200	**b.** 700	**b.** 600
4. 821	5. 197	6. 431
a. 900	**a.** 100	**a.** 500
b. 800	**b.** 200	**b.** 400
7. 345	8. 256	9. 398
a. 300	**a.** 200	**a.** 400
b. 400	**b.** 300	**b.** 300
10. 419	11. 476	12. 149
a. 500	**a.** 400	**a.** 100
b. 400	**b.** 500	**b.** 200
13. 812	14. 298	15. 111
a. 800	**a.** 300	**a.** 100
b. 900	**b.** 200	**b.** 200

Something Extra: Round the number 777 to the nearest 100. _____

Rounding Numbers

Directions: Solve each word problem. Be sure to show your work. Then, round your answer to the nearest hundred.

1. John had 57 coins in his coin collection. Matt had 87 in his coin collection. How many coins did John and Matt have together?

   Exact Answer: _____

   Rounded Answer: _____

   Show your work:

2. Macey wanted to raise money for her favorite charity. She wanted to give money to the animal shelter. She had saved 521 pennies. Her friend, Helena, said she would give Macey her pennies to give to the shelter. Helena had 398 pennies. How many pennies do Macey and Helena have to give to the shelter?

   Exact Answer: _____

   Rounded Answer: _____

   Show your work:

3. Sam had played 124 baseball games in his career. His friend, Rob, had played 223 baseball games in his career. How many total games had the two friends played in their careers?

   Exact Answer: _____

   Rounded Answer: _____

   Show your work:

4. Ken liked to count things while he rode his bicycle. He counted 33 houses, 40 trees, 15 dogs, and 33 mailboxes. How many total things did Ken count?

   Exact Answer: _____

   Rounded Answer: _____

   Show your work:

More or Less

Part 1

Directions: Look at each group. Use the less than (<) or greater than (>) signs to show which group has less or more than the other.

Example: ○○○○○ > ○○○

1.

2.

3.

4.

5.

6.

Part 2

Directions: Write two of your own greater than/less than problems. Switch problems with a friend and solve.

1. _____

2. _____

Is There More or Less?

Directions: Look at the numbers below. Use the greater than (>) or less than (<) sign to show which number is more or less than the other number.

> **Example:** 78 _<_ 128 (78 is less than 128)

1. 16_____ 38

2. 87_____ 198

3. 761_____ 129

4. 76_____ 90

5. 12_____ 10

6. 912 _____ 973

7. 91_____ 65

8. 344_____ 443

9. 22_____ 44

10. 811 _____ 106

11. 988_____ 910

12. 192_____ 291

13. 29_____ 65

14. 431_____ 512

15. 78_____ 34

16. 71_____ 54

17. 875 _____ 758

18. 376 _____ 632

19. 14_____ 12

20. 777_____ 888

21. 81_____ 18

22. 562_____ 62

Perimeter? What's That?

What is the perimeter of an object? The *perimeter* of an object is the distance around the object. To find the perimeter, you measure the sides of the object and then add the lengths together.

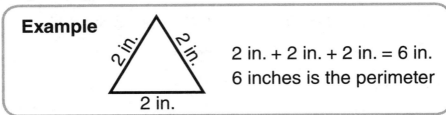

Example

2 in. + 2 in. + 2 in. = 6 in.
6 inches is the perimeter

Directions: Read and solve the following word problems to find the perimeter of each object.

1. Cal painted a picture for his art project. Each of the four sides of his canvas was 5 inches. What was the total perimeter of Cal's canvas?
   Answer:
   _____

   Show your work:

2. Melanie is getting new tile for her kitchen floor. She measured one of the square tiles. Each side of the tile measured 4 inches. What is the total perimeter of one of the square tiles Melanie will use in her kitchen?
   Answer:
   _____

   Show your work:

3. Candy was not sure if her book would fit in her backpack. She measured her book to find out. Two sides of her book measured 7 inches. The other two sides measured 11 inches. What is the total perimeter of Candy's book?
   Answer:
   _____

   Show your work:

4. Mrs. Smith bought a new picture frame. The packaging on the frame said the frame could hold a picture that is 4 inches x 6 inches. What is the total perimeter of the picture the frame can hold?
   Answer:
   _____

   Show your work:

It's My Area

The number of square units in a particular space is the area of a shape. Count the number of squares to find the area.

Example:

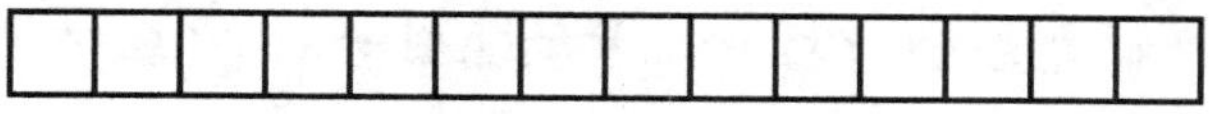

The **area** for this figure is 14 square units.

Directions: Look at each figure below. Find the area by counting the number of squares. Then, circle the letter of the correct choice.

1.

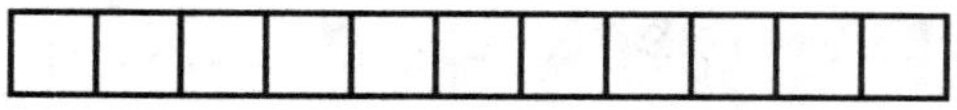

a. 15 square units

b. 11 square units

2.

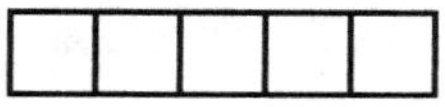

a. 5 square units

b. 3 square units

3.

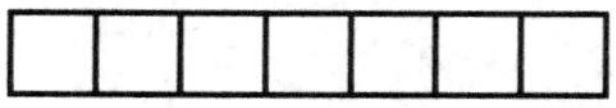

a. 6 square units

b. 7 square units

4.

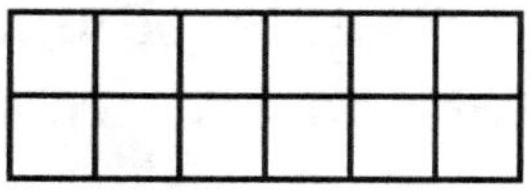

a. 10 square units

b. 12 square units

5.

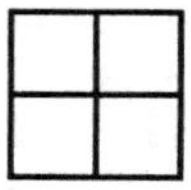

a. 4 square units

b. 3 square units

6.

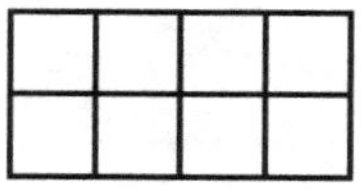

a. 9 square units

b. 8 square units

7.

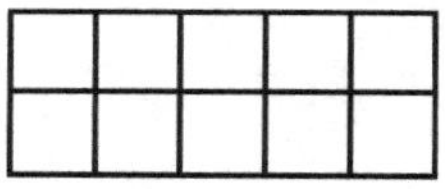

a. 8 square units

b. 10 square units

8.

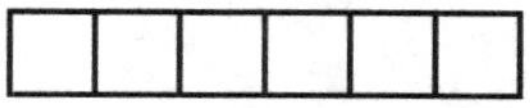

a. 6 square units

b. 16 square units

9.

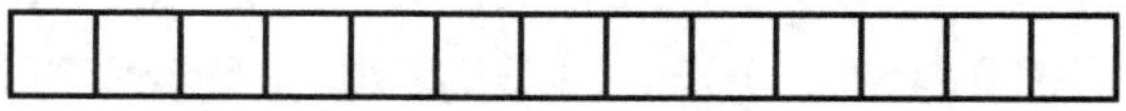

a. 12 square units

b. 13 square units

10.

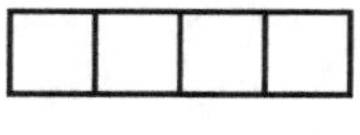

a. 5 square units

b. 4 square units

Measure the Treasure

Part 1

Directions: Use an inch ruler to help find the length of each piece that was found in the pirate's treasure chest. Write the measurement on the line.

1.

Measurement: _____

4.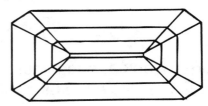

Measurement: _____

2.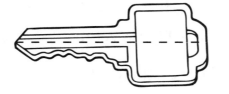

Measurement: _____

5.

Measurement: _____

3.

Measurement: _____

Part 2

Directions: Draw a picture of something that would be approximately the length that is given below. Use a ruler to help you with the measurements. Draw on another sheet of paper, if needed.

1.	3 inches			3.	2 inches
2.	1 inch	4.	5 inches		

Metric Measurement

One system of measuring is called the metric system. In the metric system, both *millimeters* and *centimeters* are used for measuring lengths. There are 10 millimeters in a centimeter.

Example

The paper clip is 5 centimeters or 50 millimeters long.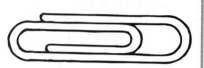

Directions: Choose the correct measurement to answer each problem. Circle the correct answer.

1. The length of this pencil is
 	
    a. 16 millimeters.
 	
    b. 6 centimeters.

	4. The length of the magic wand is
	
	    a. 25 millimeters.
	
	    b. 8 centimeters.

2. The length of the car alarm is
 	
    a. 45 millimeters.
 	
    b. 60 centimeters.
 	
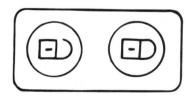
	5. The length of the book is
	
	    a. 9 millimeters.
	
	    b. 9 centimeters.
	
	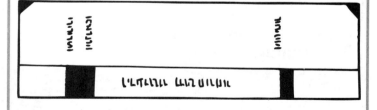

3. The length of the feather is
 	
    a. 7 centimeters.
 	
    b. 14 millimeters.

	6. The length of the friendly snake is
	
	    a. 10 centimeters.
	
	    b. 80 millimeters.

Liquid Measurement

Have you ever had to measure any liquids? When people are cooking from recipes, they often have to make liquid measurements. There are many other reasons why people might need to measure liquids.

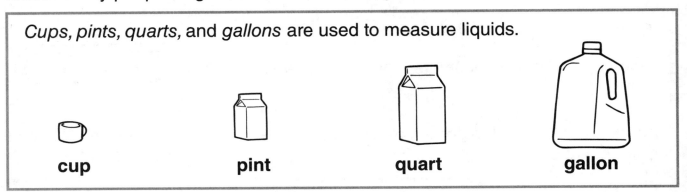

Cups, pints, quarts, and *gallons* are used to measure liquids.

cup   **pint**   **quart**   **gallon**

Directions: Color the picture that matches the liquid measurement that is given.

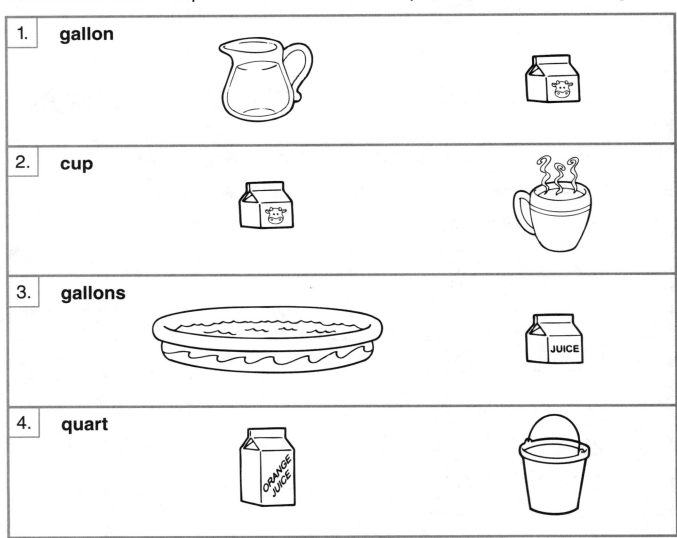

1. **gallon**

2. **cup**

3. **gallons**

4. **quart**

Measuring Liquids in Metrics

The metric system has its own units of measurement for liquid measurements. Milliliters and liters are two liquid measurements in the metric system. *Milliliters* are used to measure very small amounts of liquid. *Liters* are used to measure larger amounts of liquid. It takes 1,000 milliliters to make 1 liter!

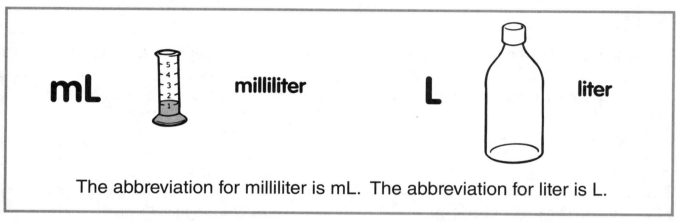

mL   milliliter   **L**   liter

The abbreviation for milliliter is mL. The abbreviation for liter is L.

Directions: Decide on the correct unit of measurement for each item listed. Write the correct measurement on the line. Would you use **mL** or **L**?

1. lemon juice for a glass of tea

   _____

2. gas for a go-cart

   _____

3. a pot of hot chocolate

   _____

4. a sip of hot cider

   _____

5. a dose of cough syrup

   _____

6. cream for a cup of coffee

   _____

7. a bathtub of water

   _____

8. water for a wading pool

   _____

9. a large pitcher of tea

   _____

10. eye drops for sore eyes

   _____

Why Weight?

Ounces and *pounds* are both units for measuring weight. It takes 16 ounces to equal 1 pound. So an ounce is much smaller than a pound. The abbreviation for the word *ounce* is **oz**. The abbreviation for the word *pound* is **lb**. How many pounds and ounces did you weigh when you were born?

Part 1

Directions: Circle the letter of the correct weight measurement for each problem.

1.	**a piece of bubble gum** **a.** ounces **b.** pounds	4.	**an ink pen** **a.** ounces **b.** pounds
2.	**a third-grade student** **a.** ounces **b.** pounds	5.	**a large bag of sugar** **a.** ounces **b.** pounds
3.	**a German shepherd** **a.** ounces **b.** pounds	6.	**a feather** **a.** ounces **b.** pounds

Part 2

Directions: In the spaces below, draw items that could be measured using the suggested measurements. Label what you have drawn on the lines provided.

Measured in ounces:	**Measured in pounds:**
_____	_____

Measuring Time

Directions: Circle the time that would be closest to the correct answer.

1. How long does it take to get a good night's sleep?

   a. seconds   **c.** hours

   b. minutes   **d.** days

2. How long does it take for a plant to grow?

   a. seconds   **c.** hours

   b. minutes   **d.** days

3. How long does it take to microwave a bag of popcorn?

   a. seconds   **c.** hours

   b. minutes   **d.** days

4. How long does it take to go through a school day?

   a. seconds   **c.** hours

   b. minutes   **d.** days

5. How long does it take to watch a movie?

   a. seconds   **c.** hours

   b. minutes   **d.** days

6. How long does it take to write your first name?

   a. seconds   **c.** hours

   b. minutes   **d.** days

Telling Time

Directions: Look at each clock. Write the correct time on the line.

1. 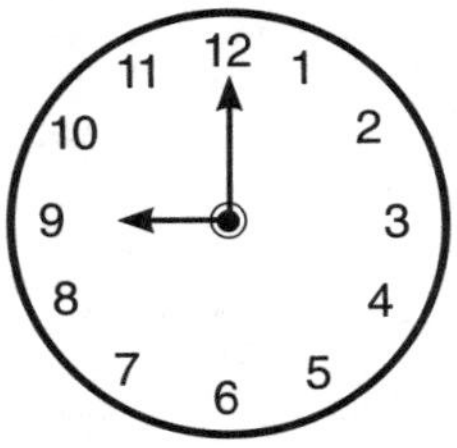

_______ : _______

2. 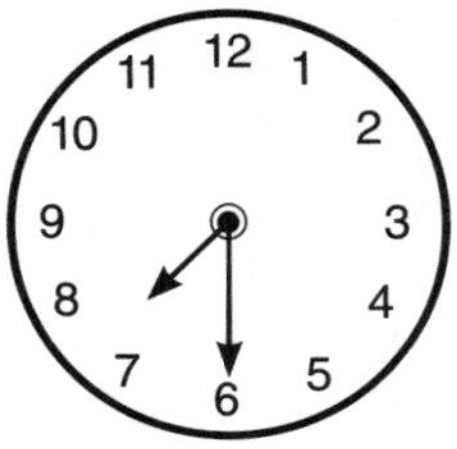

_______ : _______

3. 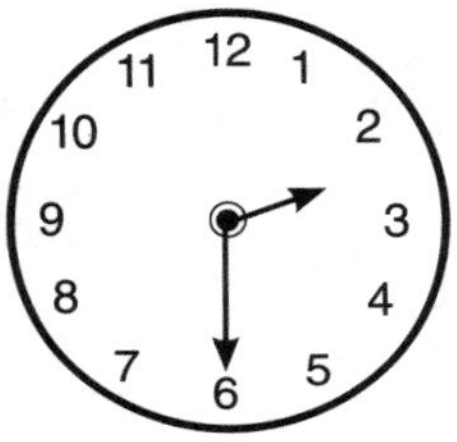

_______ : _______

4. 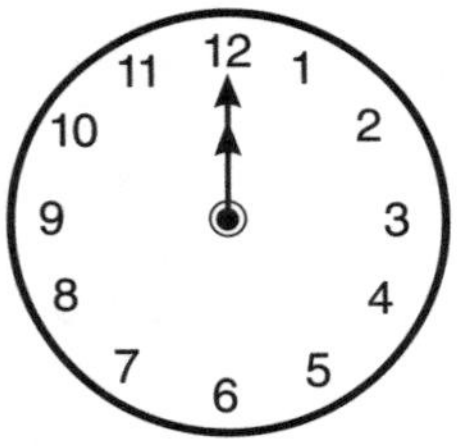

_______ : _______

5. 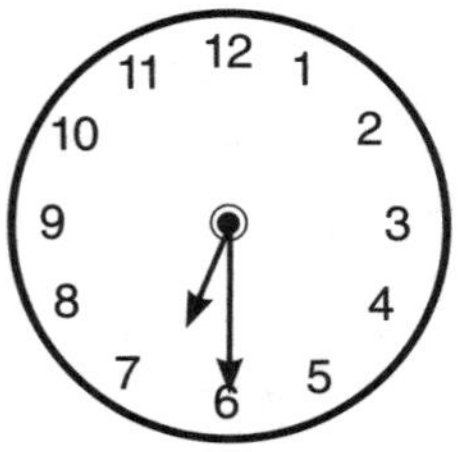

_______ : _______

6. 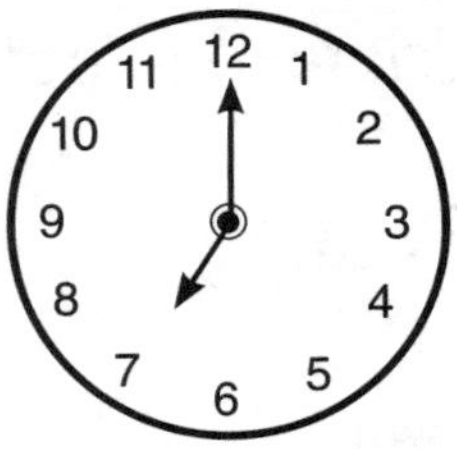

_______ : _______

7. 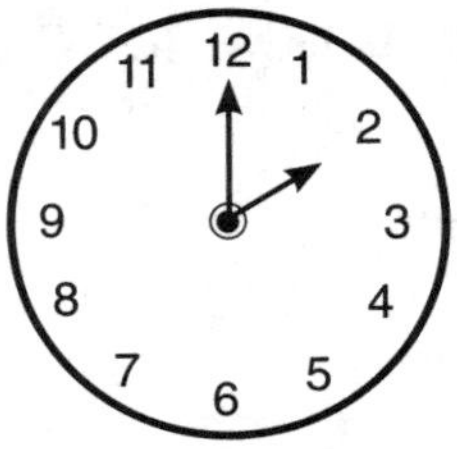

_______ : _______

8. 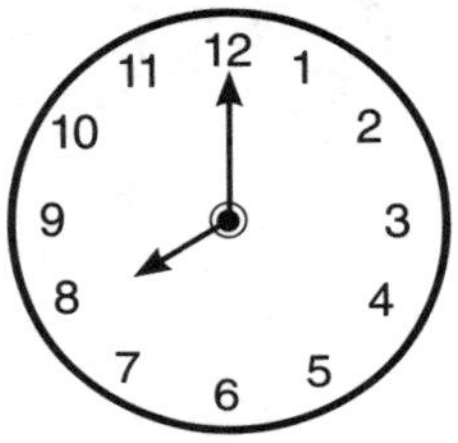

_______ : _______

9. 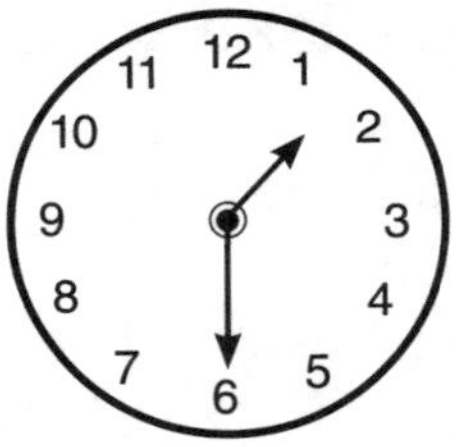

_______ : _______

10. 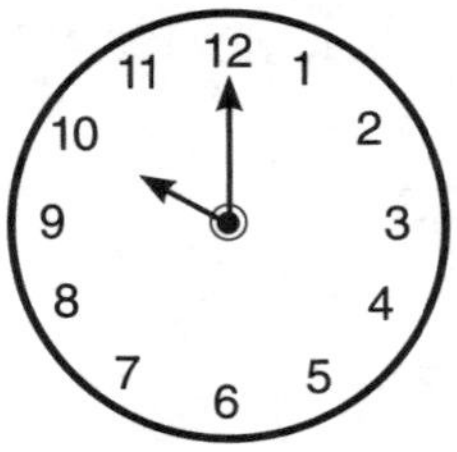

_______ : _______

Something Extra: Look at the clock on the right. Draw the hour hand and the minute hand on the clock so that the time is 3:30.

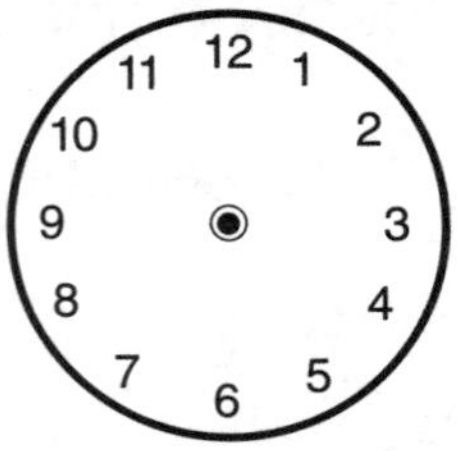

Measure by Fives to Tell Time

You can count by fives to tell time to five minutes.

The hour is seven. There are also forty-five minutes
if you count by fives. So the time on the clock is 7:45.

Hint: When you are looking at a clock, each distance between the two large
numbers shown is five minutes. So from the 12 to the 1 is five minutes. From the
1 to the 2 is five minutes. From the 2 to the 3 is five minutes, and so on.

Directions: Look at each clock. Draw in the hour hand and the minute hand to
show the time that is written.

1.   9:15

5.   1:25

2.   6:30

6.   11:40

3.   8:05

7.   7:30

4.   2:20

8.   12:20

Basic Shapes

The outline of a shape forms a *plane figure.* This means that it is a flat, two-dimensional shape.

Part 1

Directions: Trace the shape that is given. Then, draw the same shape beside the one you traced.

1. **triangle**

2. **square**

3. **circle**

4. **rectangle**

Part 2

Directions: Draw and color a picture in the space below. However, you can only use the plane figures you practiced drawing in Part I to make your work of art.

Shapes with Shape

Not all shapes are flat. Look at the shapes below, and study their names.

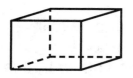

rectangular prism   cone   sphere   cylinder   cube

Part 1

Directions: Practice drawing each shape that is listed.

1.	cube	2.	cone
3.	sphere	4.	cylinder
5.	rectangular prism		

Part 2

Directions: Name the shape of each figure. Use the list of figures in *Part I* to help you name the shapes.

Picture	Shape
1. game die	_____
2. ice-cream cone	_____
3. soccer ball	_____
4. can of soup 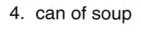	_____

Native Americans

Directions: Look at each picture. Draw a line to match each picture to the correct description.

1.

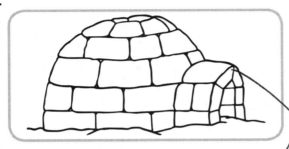

2.

3.

4.

a. The Pueblo Indians lived in homes made of adobe or stone. Adobe is clay and straw that is baked into bricks. The homes of these Indians were built into cliffs and looked like small villages or apartments.

b. The Eskimo Indians lived in cold, snowy regions. Their homes were often built out of the snow and ice. These ice shelters were called igloos.

c. The Plains Indians were nomadic Indians. The word *nomadic* means they moved frequently. Since the Plains Indians often followed their food source, they needed homes that could move easily with them. The tepee was the perfect home for these Indians.

d. The Iroquois Indians were farmers and lived in more permanent residences than some other Indian tribes. The Iroquois Indians were not a nomadic tribe. They built longhouses, which were very large and could house many people in one home.

Something Extra: Research the Native Americans of your area. Find out which Indian tribes lived in the area where you now live. What type of homes did the Indians have? On the back of this page, write down your information. Then, draw a picture to show what style home the Indians had.

Pioneers

The original pioneers often left their homes and traveled into unknown areas of the country. The brave men and women traveled by covered wagon. Some traveled alone. Many traveled with other pioneers headed out West in groups called *wagon trains*.

Part 1

Directions: Imagine you are a pioneer from the past headed out West. Circle the items that would **not** have existed in the days of the pioneers.

Part 2

Directions: Draw and color a picture of something you would want to take with you if you were a pioneer. Then, explain why you would want to take this item with you.

_____

_____

_____

_____

_____

_____

Colonial Communities

The United States began with thirteen colonies. Each colony was unique, but each one also had things in common with the others. For example, colonies in New England dealt with much colder weather than the colonies of the South, such as Georgia and South Carolina. However, both of these areas relied on the Atlantic Ocean for much of their trade and food, and all of the colonies were ruled by England.

Some of the colonists did not agree with the way England governed the colonies. Many colonists wanted to be free. They wanted to create their own country. Eventually, most of the colonists agreed to fight for freedom although some colonists did stay loyal to England. After several years of war, the thirteen colonies won their freedom. Each colony now had one major thing in common: They were part of a new nation, the United States of America.

Directions: Circle the letter of the correct answer.

1. How many colonies were there when the United States first became a country?

   a. twelve   **b.** three   **c.** thirteen

2. The original colonies had

   a. nothing in common.

   b. some things in common.

   c. everything in common.

3. According to the story, many of the colonists wanted

   a. to create their own country.

   b. to become a part of Canada.

   c. to trade with other colonists.

4. Eventually the colonists decided to fight for their

   a. right to vote.

   b. right to be a free nation.

   c. right to trade with other colonies.

Something Extra: Research and find a map of the original thirteen colonies. On the back of this page, draw a map and label each of the thirteen colonies.

Community Helpers

Community helpers are people whose jobs help people. Community helpers make a positive difference or impact in the community.

Directions: Look at the list of community helpers. On the lines provided, explain how each one might help the community in a positive way.

1. **A Crossing Guard**

keep kids safe when going to school

2. **Doctor**

make people fe

3. **Librarian**

4. **Firefighter**

Something Extra: What type of community helper would you like to be? How would you help the community? Write your answer on the back of this page.

Community Buildings

Directions: Below are some community buildings from the *present*. Use the words in the box to label them.

fire department	hospital	grocery store
police department	post office	school

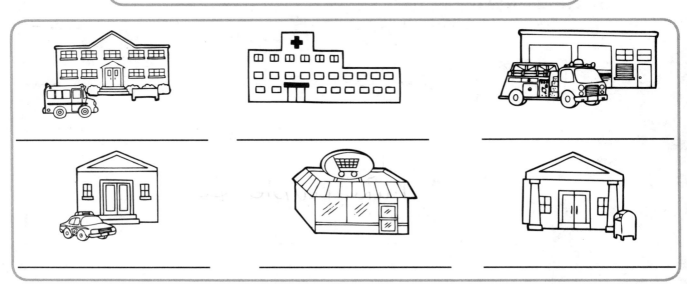

Directions: Below are some community buildings from the *past.* Use the words in the box to label them.

doctor's office	hotel	horse stable
market	school	sheriff's office

Know Your World

Directions: Use the words below to label the world map. When you are finished, color the map.

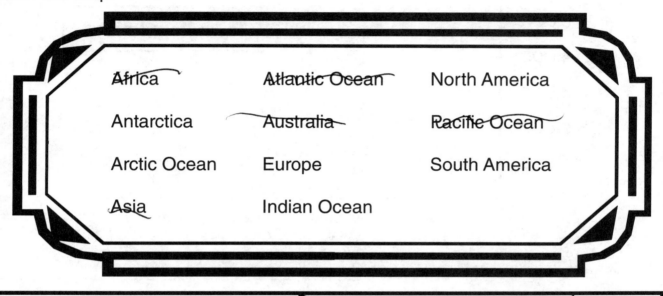

Africa   Atlantic Ocean   North America

Antarctica   Australia   Pacific Ocean

Arctic Ocean   Europe   South America

Asia   Indian Ocean

Reading a Graph

Directions: Look at the bar graph below. Answer the questions that follow.

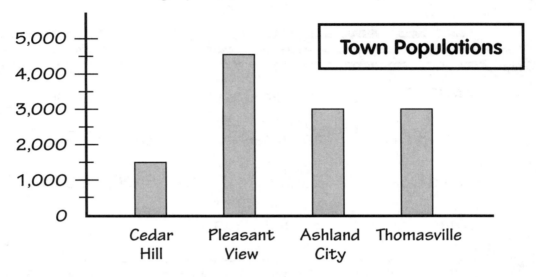

1. What is the title of this graph? _____

2. Which city has the least amount of people? _____

3. Which two cities have the same population? _____

    _____

4. Which cities have less than 5,000 people in the total population?

    _____

5. Which city has the most people living there? _____

    What is the total population of this city? _____

6. How many more people live in Pleasant View than in Cedar Hill? _____

Something Extra: Find out how many people live in your city or community.

City Name: _____   **Population:** _____

Learning About the World

A long time ago, people thought the world was flat, like a piece of paper. If people sailed too far out in the ocean, they would simply fall off the edge of the world! Of course, everyone now knows that is not true at all. The world is, in fact, shaped like a sphere or round ball. So if people started sailing out in the ocean, they wouldn't fall off the world; instead, they might circle the world . . . if they knew where they were going!

To help with locations, Earth has been divided into hemispheres. Pretend there is an imaginary line cutting Earth in two from top to bottom. This line divides Earth into two halves called the Western Hemisphere and the Eastern Hemisphere. Earth is also divided into the Northern and Southern Hemispheres. A compass rose is also used to help show direction on a map of Earth.

Directions: Answer each question.

1. Look at the compass rose. What direction is straight up? _____

2. Look at the compass rose. What direction points to the right? _____

3. Draw and label a compass rose.

4. List the four hemispheres.

   _____

   _____

   _____

   _____

5. What hemisphere do you live in? _____

6. The imaginary line that divides Earth into the Northern and Southern Hemispheres is called the equator. Is Antarctica above or below the equator?

   _____

Directions on a Map

Directions: Use the compass rose and your map skills to answer the questions below. Circle the letter of the answer that is correct.

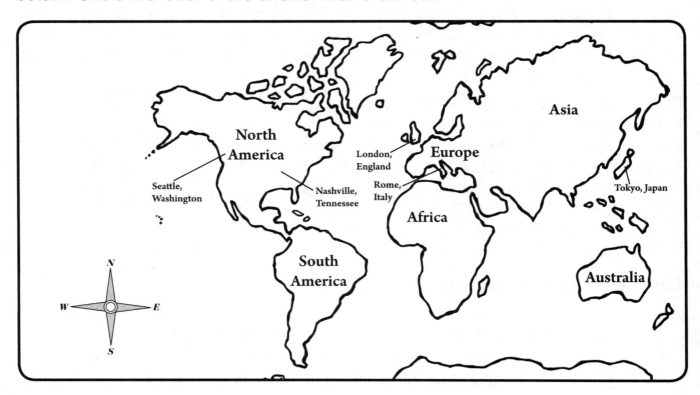

1. Rome, Italy, is located _____ of London, England.

   a. northwest   **b.** southeast

2. South America is located _____ of North America.

   a. south   **b.** west

3. Looking at this map, Africa is located _____ of South America.

   a. west   **b.** east

4. Tokyo, Japan, is _____ of Australia.

   a. north   **b.** south

5. Seattle, Washington, is _____ of Nashville, Tennessee.

   a. northeast   **b.** northwest

Understanding a Map Key

Some maps have symbols on them. To understand the symbols, study the Map Key. The symbols on the key will explain the symbols used on the map.

Directions: Study the map and map key. Answer the questions that follow.

Vacation Town Map

1. What is the title of this map? <u>vacation town map</u>

2. What does the symbol 🌲🌲🌲 stand for? <u>trees</u>

3. What does the symbol 〽️ stand for on the map? <u>mountains</u>

4. Are there houses located in the mountains? <u>yes</u>

5. Are there houses located near the water? <u>yes</u>

6. Does the town have mountains? <u>yes</u>

7. What would you add to the map?
   Draw your own symbol in the box on the
   right and then write what the symbol means.

8. Draw the symbol where you think it
   would go on the map.

Reading a Pie Graph

Directions: Use the pie graph to answer the questions.

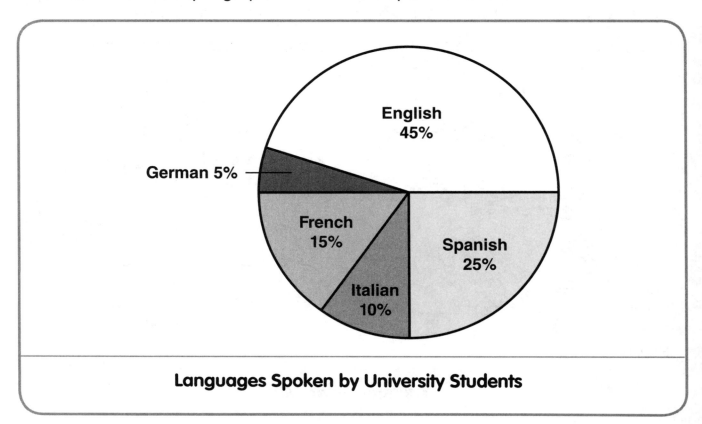

Languages Spoken by University Students

1. What percentage of the students at the university speak Italian? _____

2. Which language is the most common among the students? _____

3. Which language is spoken the least among the students? _____

4. What is the percentage of students who speak French? _____

5. How many more students speak English than Italian? _____

6. Which language is spoken by 25% of the students? _____

7. Which language is spoken by 10% of the students? _____

8. Which language or languages listed on the graph can you speak?

_____

An Important Declaration

Directions: Read the passage, and answer the questions below.

The Declaration of Independence is one of the most important documents in American history. The document was mostly written by Thomas Jefferson, but it represented the ideas of many people.

Why is the document called the Declaration of Independence? Well, the word "declare" means to state or say something. So, a declaration is something that is being said that people want other people to really listen to and hear. The word "independence" means to be free of others. In particular, this document declared that the colonists of America wanted the King of England to hear what they were saying. The colonists told the King of England that if changes were not made, then the colonists were going to declare themselves free of English rule. And that is just what they did! This document helped begin the Revolutionary War, a war that is also known as the War of Independence. Since the Declaration of Independence was officially adopted on July 4, 1776, this date would become America's birth date.

1. What does the word "declare" mean?

   _____

2. What does the word "independence" mean?

   _____

3. Who was the primary author of the Declaration of Independence?

   _____

4. Why was the Declaration of Independence written?

   _____

5. What is another name for the Revolutionary War?

   _____

6. What date is celebrated as America's birthday?

   _____

The Constitution

Directions: Read the passage, and answer the questions below.

> The thirteen colonies became independent from England at the end of the Revolutionary War. When the war was over, the new country needed an official document to help the colonies become a united nation. The document that helped unite or join the colonies together is the Constitution of the United States of America.
>
> The Declaration of Independence declared that the thirteen colonies wanted to be free of England. The Constitution told what rights Americans would have and how they would live once they were free from England. The Constitution is a written document that states the rights and freedoms the American people would have in their new country. The Constitution, though written well over two hundred years ago, can still be seen if you visit Washington D.C., the nation's capital city.

1. What was the name of the war where the thirteen colonies became independent from England? _____

2. What document helped unite or join the colonies together?

   _____

3. The Declaration of Independence declared _____

   _____

4. The Constitution of the United States of America is a written document that states _____

   _____

5. Which document do you think is more important—the Declaration of Independence or the Constitution? Explain your answer.

   _____

   _____

The Flag of America

Directions: Read the passage, and answer the questions below.

> There are many important symbols that represent a country. One of the most important symbols a country can have is its flag. The flag of the United States of America went through many changes and designs.
>
> Today's American flag has fifty stars. These stars represent the fifty states. The flag has thirteen stripes. These stripes represent the original thirteen colonies. The colors of the flag are red, white, and blue.

1. One important symbol of a country is its _____ .

2. The flag of the United States of America went through many changes and

   _____ .

3. Today's American flag has _____ stars.

4. The stars on the American flag represent the _____ .

5. There are _____ stripes on the American flag.

6. The stripes represent the original thirteen _____ .

Draw and color a picture of the flag of the United States of America.

The Pledge

One important symbol of America is the flag. When people see the flag, they sometimes think of the pledge. The pledge is an important American oath.

Directions: Read each section of the pledge. Circle the letter of the correct meaning for each part.

---

1. "pledge allegiance to the Flag"

    a. This means to be loyal to the flag and what it represents or stands for.

    b. This means not to be loyal to the flag and what it represents or stands for.

---

2. "of the United States of America"

    a. This is referring to the original thirteen colonies.

    b. This is referring to the fifty states in America.

---

3. "and to the Republic for which it stands,"

    a. This means the type of government America has, where all people have a voice in the government.

    b. This means the type of government America has, where no one has a voice in the government.

---

4. "one Nation, under God, indivisible,"

    a. This means a nation that can be divided and will not get along because the people are all just too different.

    b. This means a nation that will not be divided and people will find a way to all get along no matter their differences.

---

5. "with liberty and justice for all."

    a. This means the United States is a nation where the people will be free and treated fairly.

    b. This means the United States is a nation where no one is free and no one will be treated fairly.

State Symbols

The United States of America has many symbols that are important to the country. Some symbols that are important to America are the flag, the Statue of Liberty, the bald eagle, and the Liberty Bell.

The United States is made up of fifty individual states. Each of these states also has symbols that are important to them. When you live in a state, it is important to know its symbols. Learn more about the state where you live by answering the questions below.

Directions: Use an encyclopedia, fact book from your state, or other reference source to help find the answers to the questions below.

My State: _____

1. Does your state have a nickname? If yes, what is it? _____

   _____

2. What is your state's flower? _____

3. What is the title of your state's song?_____

4. What is your state's bird? _____

5. What is your state's animal? _____

In the spaces below, draw and color your state's flag and your state's most famous landmark or building.

flag

landmark or building

The Three Branches

Directions: Read the passage, and answer the questions below.

> The government of the United States is divided into three branches. These three branches are the legislative (Congress), executive (the President), and judicial (Supreme Court) branches.
>
> The founding fathers of the country divided the power between three branches for a very good reason. They did not want any one area to have too much power. This division of power is called the system of checks and balances. Each branch of the government can check on the other branch to make sure it is doing what is best for the country. The power of the government is divided or balanced between each branch. The founding fathers wanted to make sure there was never one person with all of the power, like the King of England, who had so much power over the original thirteen colonies.

1. The government of the United States is divided into _____ branches.

2. List the branches of the government:

    a. _____

    b. _____

    c. _____

3. Which of the three branches has the most power? Explain your answer.

    _____

    _____

4. Why did the founding fathers of the United States of America divide the power between three branches of government? _____

    _____

5. You know the United States' government is divided into three branches. Research and find out if each state government is also divided into three branches. Report your findings back to the class.

Important Americans

There have been many important people who have influenced America's history.

Directions: Match the name of the person to his or her description. Write the letter on the line provided. Use a reference source, if needed.

_____ 1. Thomas Jefferson   _____ 5. Abraham Lincoln

_____ 2. Martin Luther King, Jr.   _____ 6. Harriet Tubman

_____ 3. George Washington   _____ 7. Susan B. Anthony

_____ 4. Rosa Parks

a. This person helped begin the Civil Rights Movement. He wanted to solve social issues with peaceful protests instead of violence. He is known for his "I Have a Dream" speech where he dreamed of a world where everyone would be treated equally.

b. This person was an important figure during the Revolutionary War. He is known for writing the Declaration of Independence. He would later become the third president of the United States of America.

c. This important figure worked for women's right to vote. This is sometimes called *suffrage*. She was also the first female to ever appear on a United States' coin.

d. This person was an escaped slave. She later helped other slaves to escape to freedom on the Underground Railroad.

e. This person was an important part of the Civil Rights Movement. She would not give up her seat on the bus when she was told to move. Many people in Alabama boycotted or refused to ride the public buses to show their support of this American hero.

f. This person was president of the United States during the Civil War. He helped free the slaves in America and helped keep the South from permanently leaving the country. He was later assassinated, but he is remembered as a great president.

g. This person was a brave general during the Revolutionary War. He would later become the first president of the United States of America. His picture is on the U.S. dollar bill and the U.S. quarter.

Major Holidays

The United States has many major holidays that celebrate important American values, such as freedom and democracy. The idea of freedom is easy for us to understand. It is the idea that everyone has the right to be free, but years ago this was not such an easy idea for everyone in this country to agree on.

Democracy is also an important part of being an American. In a democratic government, everyone who is a legal citizen is able to have a say or a voice in the government. Not all countries have a democratic government, but America does.

Directions: Research each important American holiday, and write a brief description of each one. Try and find out the date of each holiday.

Hint: Some holidays do not happen on the same day of the month each year.

Martin Luther King, Jr. Day: _____

_____

Presidents' Day: _____

_____

Memorial Day: _____

_____

Independence Day: _____

_____

Labor Day: _____

_____

Veterans Day: _____

_____

Thanksgiving Day: _____

_____

Energy

Energy comes to Earth from the sun in the form of sunlight. Earth needs the energy from sunlight for many reasons.

Part 1

Directions: Circle the objects in the box that need sunlight for energy. Draw an **X** on the objects that do not need sunlight for energy.

a plant	a shoe	a tree
a birthday cake	a person	a bicycle
a garden	a couch	a solar-powered car

Part 2

Directions: People use solar energy, or energy from sunlight, to power many of the everyday things they use, such as lights and cars. Think about a world using more solar energy. Draw a picture of your school using solar energy. Explain what is being powered by the energy coming from the sunlight.

In my picture, solar energy is being used _____

_____

_____

The State of Things

Substances can be grouped into three states. These three states of matter are solids, liquids, and gases.

> *Solids* have definite shape, mass, and volume.
>   A *baseball* is an example of a solid.
>
> *Liquids* have no definite shape, but they do have mass and volume.
>   *Milk* is an example of a liquid.
>
> *Gases* have no definite shape, mass, or volume.
>   *Steam* rising from a boiling pot is an example of a gas.

Directions: Look at each picture. Label it as either a solid, a liquid, or a gas. Use the arrows to help you know which part of the picture should be labeled.

1.

_____

2.

_____

3.

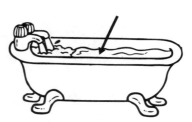

_____

4.

_____

5.

_____

6.

_____

Understanding Mass and Matter

Mass is the amount of matter in an object. Well, then, what is matter? *Matter* is made up of tiny particles. These tiny particles are called *atoms* and are too small for the naked eye to see. When these particles or atoms are packed tightly together, an object has more mass. An object will weigh more if it has more mass.

Directions: Look at each picture. Write down the name of the picture. Then, draw a picture that would have more mass than what is already pictured. Write the name of what you have drawn underneath the new picture.

Example:

frog   horse

1.

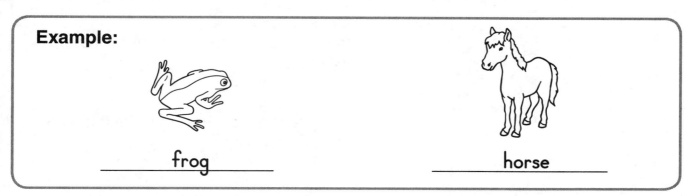

_____   _____

2.

_____   _____

3.

_____   _____

Defining the Words

Directions: Match each word to its correct definition. Write the correct letter on the line.

Words	Definitions
_____ 1. atoms	**a.** an example of a gas
_____ 2. mass	**b.** tiny particles, too small for the naked eye to see
_____ 3. solid	**c.** a state of matter that has definite shape, mass, and volume
_____ 4. water	**d.** a state of matter that has no definite shape but does have mass and volume
_____ 5. liquid	**e.** a state of matter with no definite shape, mass, or volume
_____ 6. gas	**f.** how large or small something is
_____ 7. state	**g.** the form of something
_____ 8. size	**h.** an example of a liquid
_____ 9. ice	**i.** an example of a solid
_____ 10. steam	**j.** the amount of matter in an object

Speed and Motion

When objects move, we use certain terms to describe this motion.

When an object is in *motion*, it is changing positions.

Speed is a measure of the object's rate of motion. Speed refers to the time it takes an object to travel a certain distance.

Directions: Read each statement. If the statement is true, write the word "true" on the line. If the statement is false, write the word "false" on the line.

_____ 1. All objects are in motion.

_____ 2. When an object moves faster, its speed is slowing down.

_____ 3. Speed is used as a measurement to see how fast an object is moving.

_____ 4. When an object is still, it is in motion.

_____ 5. If something moves, it is in motion.

_____ 6. A parked car is in motion.

_____ 7. A car moving at 40 mph has a greater speed than a car moving at 30 mph.

_____ 8. Motion stops when an object is still.

Something Extra: On the back of this page, draw and color a picture of something that is not in motion and something that is in motion.

The Forces of Push and Pull

When you push something, you move it. When you pull something, you move it. *Pushing* and *pulling* are both forces of motion. When an object is very light, it takes little force to move it. When an object is heavy, it takes a lot of force to move it. When an object needs to be moved, someone must decide if it would be easier to move the object by pulling it or pushing it. For example, it is easier to push a bike with a flat tire than to pull the bike. But, it is usually easier to pull a wagon than it is to push it.

Directions: Look at each picture below. Write the word "push" if you would most often push the object to move it. Write the word "pull" if you would most often pull the object to move it.

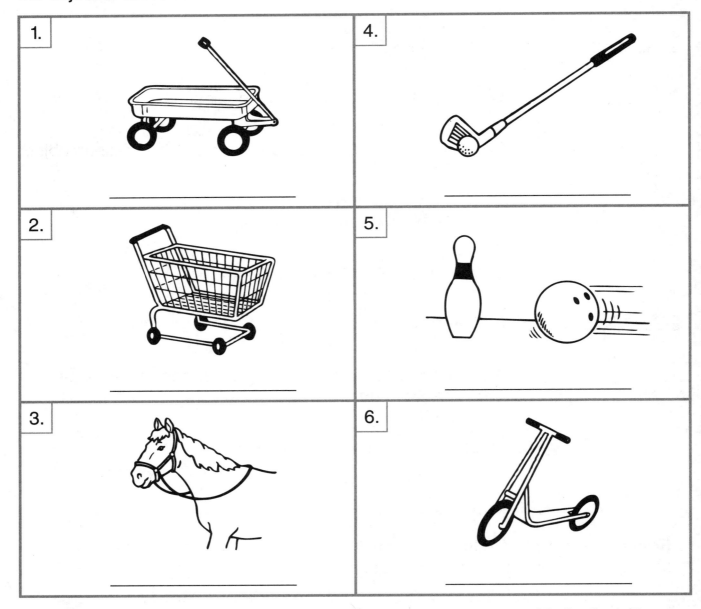

Gravity: The Ultimate Force

Gravity is one of the most important forces in our universe. *Gravity* is the invisible force that pulls objects towards Earth. The moon, for example, is held in orbit by Earth's gravitational pull. However, the further away an object is, the less gravity acts as a force on the object. The moon is so far away from Earth that gravity does not pull the moon into Earth. Thank goodness!

Gravity is important to you, too, in your everyday life. Think about what happens when you are playing outside. If you pick up a ball and throw it up into the air, it doesn't float away. The ball falls back to the ground. This is gravity in action that you can see.

Directions: Answer each question.

1. Gravity is an invisible _____ .

2. Gravity pulls objects _____ Earth.

3. The moon is held in _____ by Earth's gravitational pull.

4. The _____ away an object is, the less gravity acts as a force on the object.

5. Gravity does not pull the moon into Earth because the moon is so

   _____ _____.

6. If you throw a ball up into the air, _____ will pull the ball back to the ground.

Something Extra: In the space below, draw and color a picture of yourself at school, but on a day where there is no gravity in action!

All About Environment

Environment is important to all living things. All living things, plants, and animals must adapt to their environment. A *camel* is a good example of an animal adapting to its environment. A camel must be able to store water for long periods of time because the camel lives in a very dry environment. The camel knows that once it finds water, it may not find water again for a very long time. This is because a camel lives in the desert, which is a very dry place.

Directions: Circle the correct answer. Write the correct answer on the line.

1. All living things must _____ .

   a. fight against their environment.

   b. adapt to their environments.

2. An animal that survives by storing water for use during dry periods is the

   _____ .

   a. horse   **b.** camel

3. Environment is necessary to _____ .

   a. everything that is alive.   **b.** nothing.

4. A _____ is an example of a very dry environment.

   a. forest   **b.** desert

Different Places

Different plants and animals live in different environments.

Part 1

Directions: Write a definition or description of each environment.

Ocean: _____

_____

_____

Desert: _____

_____

_____

Forest: _____

_____

_____

Grassland: _____

_____

_____

Part 2

Directions: Think of an animal that would live in each environment. Draw each animal in the correct environment above.

Food Chains

Living things need food to make energy. *Producers* are living things that can make their own food. *Consumers* are living things that cannot make their own food. There are several types of consumers. Consumers are known as herbivores, carnivores, and omnivores. *Herbivores* get energy from only eating plants. *Carnivores* get energy from only eating animals. *Omnivores* get energy from eating both plants and animals.

Another type of consumer is a decomposer. *Decomposers* break down and consume, or eat, dead plants and animals.

All of these living things create a food chain. The *food chain* explains how living things get the food they need to make energy.

Part 1

Directions: Define each word.

1. herbivores: _____

2. carnivores: _____

3. omnivores: _____

4. decomposers: _____

5. producers: _____

6. consumers: _____

7. food chain: _____

Part 2

Directions: List two things that each animal below might eat to get energy.

1.

a. _____

b. _____

2.

a. _____

b. _____

3.

a. _____

b. _____

The Amazing Water Cycle

The water cycle allows life to continue on Earth. Living things need water to survive. Water moves in a continuous cycle from Earth to the sky and back again. This constant movement is called the *water cycle*. The major parts of the water cycle are evaporation, condensation, precipitation, and runoff.

Evaporation is when water changes from liquid to vapor. The sun pulls the water from Earth and evaporates the liquid into the atmosphere. *Condensation* is when the water vapor changes back into liquid in the clouds. *Precipitation* is when the water falls from the clouds onto Earth. Finally, *runoff* is when the water that is not absorbed collects into watery areas such as lakes, seas, and oceans. Then, amazingly, the entire cycle starts again!

Directions: Below is a picture of the water cycle. The parts of the cycle are not labeled. Write the correct names on the lines in the picture. Color the picture when you are finished.

Parts of the Water Cycle

| condensation | evaporation | precipitation | runoff |

Life Changes

Because Earth has changed over the years, the plants and animals that live on Earth have also changed. One way to learn about plants and animals of the past is to study fossils. *Fossils* are imprints, or the remains, of something that lived long ago. A scientist that studies fossils is called a *paleontologist.*

Fossils can be found in many different shapes and sizes. They are often found in the layers of Earth's rocks and soil. Some fossils are even found in the hardened amber that comes from trees. Wherever they are found, fossils give us a look at the plants and animals that lived long ago.

Part 1

Directions: Write down five facts you learned from reading the paragraphs above about fossils.

1. _____

2. _____

3. _____

4. _____

5. _____

Part 2

Directions: Look at the fossils below. Write what you think each fossil might be.

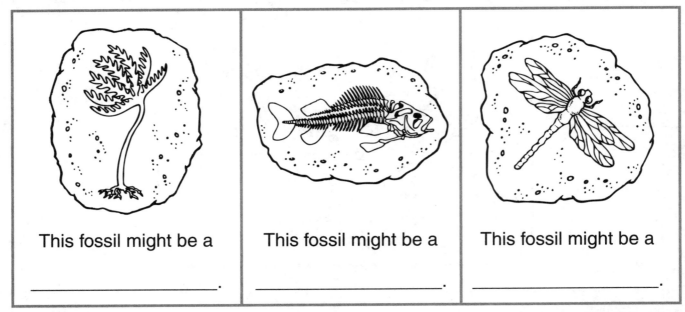

This fossil might be a

_____.

This fossil might be a

_____.

This fossil might be a

_____.

Phases and Changes

Our planet Earth orbits the sun. Our moon orbits planet Earth. Both orbits are very important.

Night and day on Earth is caused by Earth's rotation on its axis. As Earth turns, the part of Earth facing the sun has day. The part of Earth not facing the sun has night. The sun, the moon, and the rotation of Earth all help create our days and nights.

As the moon orbits Earth, something special also happens. The moon appears to change shapes. The changes are called the *phases of the moon*. Of course, the moon does not really change its shape. The shape only appears to change because the moon is receiving different amounts of light from the sun.

Part 1

Directions: Use the passage above to answer the questions.

1. Earth orbits the _____.

2. The moon orbits _____.

3. Night and day are caused by Earth's rotation on its _____.

4. As Earth turns, the part of Earth facing the sun has _____.

5. The part of Earth that is facing away from the sun does not have day but instead has _____.

Part 2

Directions: You have read about the phases of the moon. In the space below, draw a picture of a quarter moon and a full moon. Use a reference source, if needed.

quarter moon	full moon

Our Solar System

Did you know Earth is only one planet in our solar system? Our *solar system* is, in fact, made up of the sun and all of the objects that orbit the sun. There are eight planets in our solar system. Some scientists divide the planets into two groups known as the inner and outer planets. The *inner planets* are the planets that are closest to the sun. These planets are Mercury, Venus, Earth, and Mars. The *outer planets* are the planets that are not as close to the sun. These planets are Jupiter, Saturn, Uranus, and Neptune.

Planet Earth is where you live. *Earth* is an inner planet because it is close to the sun. Earth rotates, or spins, on its axis. It takes the planet twenty-four hours or one day to complete a rotation. Earth's moon is also part of the solar system. The shape of the moon appears to change based on the amount of light it gets from the sun, but, really, its shape doesn't change at all!

Directions: Read each statement. If the statement is true, color the planet. If the statement is false, do not color the planet.

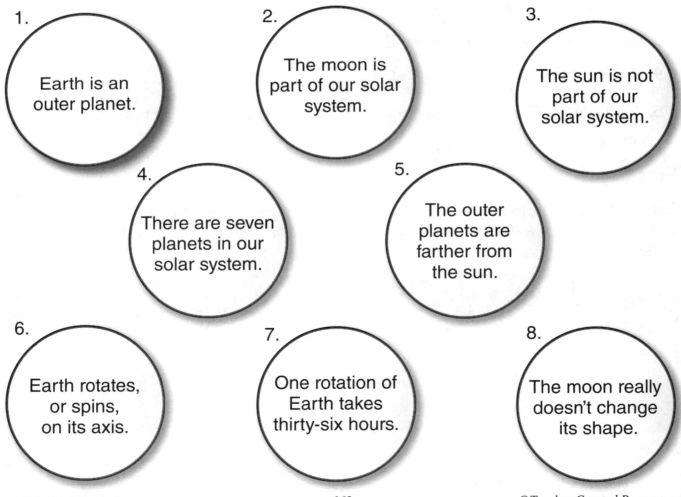

1. Earth is an outer planet.

2. The moon is part of our solar system.

3. The sun is not part of our solar system.

4. There are seven planets in our solar system.

5. The outer planets are farther from the sun.

6. Earth rotates, or spins, on its axis.

7. One rotation of Earth takes thirty-six hours.

8. The moon really doesn't change its shape.

The Inner and Outer Planets

Part 1

Directions: Below are the four inner planets drawn in order from the sun. Answer the questions that follow the picture.

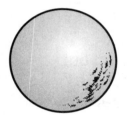   

Mercury   **Venus**   **Earth**   **Mars**

1. How many planets are between Earth and the sun? _____

2. Which planet is closest to the sun? _____

3. Would anyone be able to live on Mercury? Explain your answer.

_____

Part 2

Directions: Below are the four outer planets drawn in order from the sun. Answer the questions that follow the picture.

 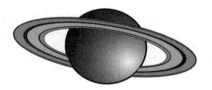  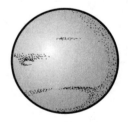

Jupiter   **Saturn**   **Uranus**   **Neptune**

1. Which planet would be coldest because of its distance from the sun?

_____

2. Which planet is known for the rings that circle it? _____

3. Which planet is third of the outer planets?_____

All in the Procedure

Scientists learn by investigating or experimenting. To conduct an experiment, the scientists must first have a question that they want answered. Then, they must form a *hypothesis,* or an educated guess, about what they think will happen at the end of the experiment. Then, they must form a *procedure,* or an experiment, to see if their question can be answered. Finally, after doing the experiment, they must reach a *conclusion,* or a result. Sometimes the scientists will find out their hypothesis was all wrong. But sometimes they will find out their hypothesis was correct. Either way, the scientists are always learning about their world.

Directions: Imagine that you have two bowls. One bowl is plastic. One bowl is glass. You also have four equal-sized blocks of ice. Think of an experiment you could conduct using the ice and the two bowls. Use the form below to set up your pretend experiment. Imagine the results of the experiment and then respond below.

Question: _____

Hypothesis: I think the following will happen: _____

_____

_____

Procedure: I tried to prove my hypothesis by doing the following procedure:

_____

_____

_____

_____

My **conclusion** after following the above procedure was that my hypothesis was/ was not correct. I know this because _____

_____

Something Extra: Conduct your experiments. Was your imagined conclusion correct? _____ Explain your answer on the back.

Reading the Charts

Directions: Read the graph and the data below to answer each question.

The following high school students were involved in an experiment to see if the number of hours of sleep they got each night helped them to earn better grades.

Look over the chart and the information to see if sleep made a difference with their grades at school.

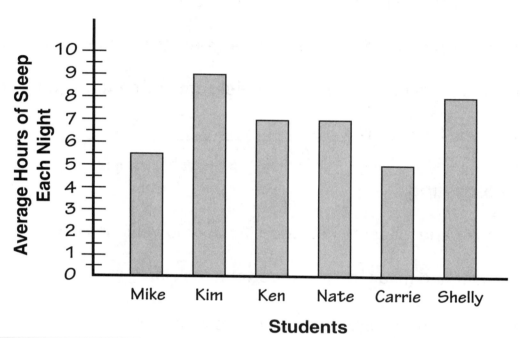

- Nate earned all Bs.
- Kim earned As and Bs.
- Mike earned Bs and Cs.
- Shelly earned all As.
- Ken earned Bs and Cs.
- Carrie earned all Cs.

After looking at the graph and the other information, what can you can conclude about the students' sleep habits and their grades? Write your conclusion below. Explain your answer.

Conclusion: _____

_____

_____

_____

_____

Using Numbers in Science

Scientists often have to use numerical data in their experiments. Use the exercise below to help practice using numerical data.

Part 1: Counting

1. Count and list how many students are in your class. _____

2. Count and list how many students sit at your table in the lunchroom. _____

3. Where are there more students? **classroom lunch table** (Circle one.)

   How do you know this? _____

Part 2: Measuring

1. Use a ruler and measure how wide the door to your classroom is. _____

2. Use a ruler and measure how wide your desk is._____

3. If your desk were double its width, would it be able to fit through the door

   of the classroom? How do you know this? _____

   _____

4. Think of something else in the classroom you could measure. What is it

   you are going to measure?_____

   What is the measurement of the object? _____

5. Think of one reason why the measurement of this object might be

   important to know. _____

   _____

The Candle Experiment

Brett wanted to do an experiment for his science fair project. He decided to see if the color of candles affected the burning rate of the candles.

In Brett's hypothesis, he believed white candles, with no color, would burn faster than candles with color.

---

1. What supplies would Brett need to conduct his experiment?

Brett's supplies:

_____

_____

_____

---

2. What would Brett need to do to conduct his experiment?

_____

_____

_____

_____

---

3. After conducting his experiment twice, Brett found out that white candles burn quicker than candles with color. Why do you think Brett conducted his experiment twice when he proved his hypothesis after the first experiment?

_____

_____

Answer Key for Third Grade

Page 34

Part 2

1. two   2. six   3. zero   4. four

Page 36

Proper Nouns	**Common Nouns**
1. Monday	holiday
2. Tammy	friend, girl
3. Bella	cake
4. Leo, Leiana	kittens
5. Helena	book, television
6. Terrell	pizza, supper
7. Christmas, Hanukkah, December	month
8. Sophie	monkey, zoo
9. Ben	star
10. Shannon	teacher, story
11. Kelly	movie
12. Tristan	mouse

Page 37

Part 1

1. crab   4. apple   2. foxes
2. car   *Part 2*   3. balloons
3. monkey 1. flowers   4. frogs

Page 38

1. He   5. friend   9. family
2. Katie   6. They   10. Summer
3. radio   7. Rabbits
4. game   8. I

Page 39

Answers will vary for both sections.

Page 40

1. past   5. future   9. past
2. present 6. present 10. present
3. past   7. past
4. present 8. future

Page 41

Answers will vary.

Page 42

Answers will vary.

Page 43

Part 1

1. very   3. tomorrow   5. so
2. slowly   4. there   6. never

Part 2

Answers will vary.

Page 44

Part 1

1. and
2. or
3. but
4. yet
5. for

Part 2

1. and
2. but
3. or
4. nor
5. so

Page 45

Sentences without double negatives:

2, 3, 5, 6, 7, 8

Page 46

Part 1

Words with prefixes or suffixes: curiosity, revisit, disappear, awaken, transform, shipment

Part 2

Answers will vary—redo, overdo, restate, statement, misstate, oversleep, enlist, relist

Page 47

Part 1

ant, book, boy, cup, happy, horse, money, paper, quiet, shirt, summer, tent

Part 2

Answers will vary.

Page 48

1. didn't *or* can't   6. weren't
2. he's   7. It's
3. don't   8. didn't *or* can't
4. hasn't   9. She's
5. should've   10. aren't

Page 49

Answers will vary for both sections.

Page 50

1. "Our   5. "I   9. "Do
2. "Does   6. "Red   10. "My
3. "My   7. "I   11. "Can
4. "Please 8. "When 12. "Today

Page 51

Part 1

1. !   2. ?   3. .   4. .   5. !   6. ?

Part 2

Answers will vary.

Page 52

Answers will vary.

Answer Key for Third Grade *(cont.)*

Page 53

1. We ordered pizza, spaghetti, and lasagna.
2. My favorite sports are basketball, soccer, and swimming.
3. I wish I could have a dog, a cat, and a gerbil for my pets.
4. C
5. For class I need paper, a pencil, and a book.
6. C
7. My favorite months are February, March, and April.
8. Mercury, Venus, and Earth are the planets that are closest to the sun.
9. We have music class on Monday, Tuesday, and Wednesday.
10. We need to get milk, bread, and cheese from the grocery store.

Something Extra: Answers will vary.

Page 54 Answers will vary.

Page 55

1. "I wish I had three wishes," Allison said.
2. "What would you do with three wishes?" Kristen asked.
3. "First, I would wish for a lot of toys," Allison said.
4. "What would you wish for next?" Kristen asked.
5. "I would wish for some toys for you, too," Allison replied.
6. "That is so nice!" Kristen exclaimed.
7. "I can be nice," Allison said.
8. "What would you wish for with your final wish?" Kristen asked.
9. "Oh, that's easy," Allison said.
10. Then, Allison added, "I would wish that you would want to give all of your new toys to me!"

Something Extra: Answers will vary but must have quotation marks.

Page 56

1. C
2. "Do you know what time it is?" Thomas asked.
3. "My dog chased my cat up a tree," Kelly said.
4. "Would you pass the ketchup, please?" Cara asked.
5. C
6. "Go get me a milkshake," Jake demanded.
7. C
8. Chloe said, "I wish today was my birthday."

9. C
10. Amanda said, "I can't come to your party."

Page 57

Part 1

1. 12:00 noon
2. 8:30 in the evening
3. 6:30 in the morning
4. 5:00 PM

Part 2

Answers will vary.

Page 58

190 Elm Street
Anytown, **K**ansas 43718
August 26, 2010

Dear Ella,

How are you? I am doing well. I miss seeing you each day like we did at camp. Camp was really a lot of fun! *(or ,)*

Please write me over the school year. I will write you back. I am going to make a scrapbook using all of our pictures. I will send you copies of the photos.

Your friend,
Linda

Page 59

Part 1

1. a   2. a   3. a   4. b   5. b

Part 2

Answers will vary.

Page 60

1. their	4. too	7. too
2. their	5. They're	8. their
3. It's	6. to	9. two

Something Extra: Answers will vary.

Page 61

1. a	3. a or b	5. a
2. a	4. a	6. b

Something Extra: Answers will vary.

Page 62 Answers will vary.

Page 63

1. b	3. a	5. b	7. b
2. a	4. a	6. a	8. a

Page 64 Answers will vary.

Page 65

1. 3rd person
2. 1st person
3. 2nd person
4. 3rd person
5. 1st person

Answer Key for Third Grade *(cont.)*

Page 66

1. a   3. b   5. b   7. b
2. b   4. b   6. a   8. a

Page 67 Answers will vary but might include:

1. moo   4. tweet *or* chirp   7. roar
2. woof   5. baa   8. meow
3. quack   6. oink

Page 68 Answers will vary.

Page 69

1. simile   6. metaphor
2. onomatopoeia   7. onomatopoeia
3. alliteration   8. onomatopoeia
4. alliteration   9. alliteration
5. simile   10. metaphor

Something Extra: Answers will vary.

Page 70

1. a   3. b   5. b
2. a   4. a   6. a

Page 71

1. a   2. b   3. b   4. b

Something Extra: Answers will vary.

Page 72

1. table of contents   3. glossary   5. index
2. glossary   4. glossary

Page 73 Answers will vary.

Page 74 Answers will vary.

Page 75

1. even   3. even   5. odd   7. odd
2. even   4. odd   6. even   8. odd

Page 76

1. 4   3. 6   5. 2   7. 9   9. 8
2. 10   4. 10   6. 7   8. 3

Page 77

Each answer will be the same for both problems.

1. 6   3. 11   5. 12   7. 8   9. 4
2. 10   4. 9   6. 17   8. 13   10. 14

Page 78

1. 22   4. 31   7. 43   10. 68   13. 20
2. 28   5. 73   8. 55   11. 41   14. 70
3. 45   6. 85   9. 75   12. 35   15. 99

Page 79

1. 818   4. 871   7. 873   10. 888
2. 962   5. 699   8. 922   11. 967
3. 765   6. 818   9. 840   12. 410

Page 80

Part 1

1. 512   4. 955   7. 555   10. 934
2. 707   5. 918   8. 660   11. 912
3. 889   6. 989   9. 922   12. 1010

Part 2

1. 853 pennies   2. 456 students   3. 786 cans

Page 81

1. 39.30   7. 5.5   13. 10.79
2. 99.45   8. 66.36   14. 47.35
3. 72.72   9. 9.23   15. 8.9
4. 29.36   10. 8.8   16. 55.55
5. 16.0   11. 87.30
6. 38.53   12. 91.19

Page 82

1. 33.54   6. 28.28   11. 11.5
2. 29.18   7. 81.18   12. 51.85
3. 97.11   8. 69.41   13. 60.53
4. 94.44   9. 24.14   14. 79.97
5. 54.99   10. 100.39

Page 83

1. $9.95   4. 61 students
2. 97 stuffed animals   5. 110 stamps
3. 100 eggs

Page 84

1. 13 songs   3. 88 keys
2. 6 members   4. 13 students

Page 85

1. 3   4. 1   7. 2   10. 2
2. 4   5. 6   8. 7   11. 2
3. 4   6. 2   9. 1   12. 0

Page 86

1. 2   6. 30   11. 55   16. 46
2. 42   7. 22   12. 4   17. 11
3. 60   8. 34   13. 50   18. 30
4. 10   9. 11   14. 71   19. 20
5. 10   10. 54   15. 1   20. 4

Page 87

Part 1

1. 33   3. 55   5. 51   7. 30   9. 21
2. 5   4. 1   6. 11   8. 1   10. 13

Part 2

1. 31¢   2. 23 pages

Answer Key for Third Grade (cont.)

Page 88

1. 7	5. 21	9. 29	13. 9
2. 45	6. 9	10. 56	14. 8
3. 48	7. 5	11. 37	15. 2
4. 2	8. 36	12. 10	16. 33

Page 89

1. 158	6. 40	11. 444	16. 693
2. 585	7. 91	12. 22	17. 131
3. 287	8. 493	13. 35	18. 6
4. 380	9. 600	14. 99	19. 308
5. 125	10. 21	15. 4	20. 595

Page 90

1. 527	6. 640	11. 889	16. 89
2. 110	7. 244	12. 311	17. 109
3. 111	8. 100	13. 77	18. 221
4. 766	9. 271	14. 30	
5. 118	10. 235	15. 56	

Page 91

1. 114	4. 221	7. 26	10. 73	13. 198
2. 6	5. 307	8. 59	11. 51	14. 20
3. 46	6. 91	9. 5	12. 4	

Page 92

1. 4.3	4. 44.1	7. 2.1	10. 48.2
2. 2.2	5. 1.1	8. 22.1	11. 3.5
3. 10.0	6. 5.4	9. 1.1	12. 1.01

Page 93

1. 312.07	5. 114.41	9. 273.12	13. 65.11
2. 15.99	6. 245.97	10. 254.00	14. 55.89
3. 429.00	7. 92.89	11. 100.00	15. 62.09
4. 22.44	8. 361.80	12. 169.71	16. 101.10

Page 94

1. 56 fish   2. 160 butterflies   3. $200.66

Page 95

1. 40	6. 26	11. 45	16. 31
2. 6	7. 63	12. 35	17. 97
3. 14	8. 75	13. 77	18. 26
4. 101	9. 64	14. 52	19. 2
5. 12	10. 6	15. 65	20. 83

Page 96

Each answer will be the same for both problems.

1. 6	5. 40	9. 42	13. 40
2. 8	6. 21	10. 8	14. 33
3. 15	7. 63	11. 16	
4. 6	8. 20	12. 27	

Page 97

1. 3	5. 24	9. 72	13. 40
2. 21	6. 60	10. 6	14. 28
3. 16	7. 32	11. 0	
4. 25	8. 42	12. 33	

Page 98

1. 4	16	6. 6	42
2. 5	30	7. 8	16
3. 7	21	8. 10	40
4. 3	24	9. 9	63
5. 2	18	10. 7	28

Page 99

1. 4	20	6. 3	21
2. 7	56	7. 8	24
3. 2	8	8. 5	55
4. 9	90	9. 1	5
5. 6	36	10. 4	32

Page 100

1. 5	15	10. 6	18
2. 3	21	11. 5	20
3. 11	44	12. 4	28
4. 5	50	13. 7	56
5. 4	12	14. 10	30
6. 4	8	15. 3	6
7. 2	10	16. 5	35
8. 9	36	17. 2	4
9. 8	72	18. 10	70

Page 101

1. 12	5. 2	9. 9	13. 9
2. 12	6. 5	10. 7	14. 8
3. 2	7. 7	11. 7	15. 8
4. 5	8. 5	12. 7	16. 6

Page 102

1. a	4. c	7. c	10. a
2. b	5. b	8. a	
3. c	6. b	9. c	

Page 103

1. 39 R1	9. 13 R3
2. 8 R7	10. 2 R4
3. 5 R1	11. 13 R3
4. 10 R1	12. 2 R2
5. 12 R1	13. 6 R1
6. 3 R1	14. 11 R4
7. 24 R3	15. 3 R2
8. 4 R2	16. 9 R3

Answer Key for Third Grade *(cont.)*

Page 104

1. 2
2. 29
3. 6
4. 15 R2
5. 8
6. 46 R1
7. 18
8. 3 R3
9. 8 R1

Page 105

1. 9 pieces   2. 50 cards   3. 3 pencils   4. 11 cars

Page 106

1. 50
2. 42
3. 9
4. 18
5. 2
6. 2
7. 8
8. 6
9. 10
10. 5
11. 8
12. 64
13. 4
14. 90
15. 9
16. 4
17. 2
18. 3
19. 144
20. 110

Page 107

1. b   2. a   3. b

Page 108

1. $\frac{7}{10}$ 2. $\frac{1}{5}$ 3. $\frac{3}{10}$ 4. $\frac{9}{10}$ 5. $\frac{2}{5}$

Page 109

1. $\frac{2}{5}$ 3. $\frac{7}{9}$ 5. $\frac{9}{12}$

2. $\frac{5}{8}$ 4. $\frac{6}{7}$ 6. $\frac{4}{6}$

Page 110

1. $\frac{8}{9}$ 5. $\frac{7}{8}$ 9. $\frac{3}{4}$ 13. $\frac{7}{9}$

2. $\frac{3}{5}$ 6. $\frac{2}{4}$ 10. $\frac{6}{12}$ 14. $\frac{11}{12}$

3. $\frac{10}{12}$ 7. $\frac{2}{3}$ 11. $\frac{4}{5}$ 15. $\frac{4}{5}$

4. $\frac{3}{3}$ 8. $\frac{9}{10}$ 12. $\frac{3}{7}$ 16. $\frac{4}{6}$

Page 111

1. $\frac{1}{5}$ 5. $\frac{3}{8}$ 9. $\frac{2}{5}$ 13. $\frac{5}{10}$

2. $\frac{1}{9}$ 6. $\frac{1}{3}$ 10. $\frac{4}{9}$ 14. $\frac{1}{4}$

3. $\frac{3}{7}$ 7. $\frac{3}{10}$ 11. $\frac{1}{8}$ 15. $\frac{1}{10}$

4. $\frac{1}{4}$ 8. $\frac{2}{12}$ 12. $\frac{4}{11}$ 16. $\frac{4}{8}$

Page 112

1. addition $\frac{3}{4}$ 10. addition $\frac{9}{12}$

2. addition $\frac{2}{9}$ 11. $\frac{2}{4}$

3. $\frac{4}{8}$ 12. $\frac{2}{5}$

4. addition $\frac{4}{5}$ 13. addition $\frac{2}{3}$

5. $\frac{5}{9}$ 14. $\frac{3}{8}$

6. $\frac{1}{4}$ 15. addition $\frac{7}{10}$

7. addition $\frac{11}{12}$ 16. addition $\frac{4}{6}$

8. $\frac{1}{11}$ 17. $\frac{3}{12}$

9. addition $\frac{4}{6}$ 18. addition $\frac{6}{7}$

Answer Key for Third Grade *(cont.)*

Page 113

1. 320 ↓
2. 680 ↑
3. 810 ↓
4. 120 ↓
5. 180 ↑
6. 560 ↓
7. 420 ↓
8. 280 ↑
9. 490 ↑
10. 530 ↓
11. 230 ↓
12. 860 ↑
13. 510 ↓
14. 750 ↑
15. 360 ↑
16. 610 ↓
17. 620 ↓
18. 710 ↑
19. 490 ↑
20. 330 ↓

Page 114

1. a   4. b   7. a   10. b   13. a
2. a   5. b   8. b   11. b   14. a
3. b   6. b   9. a   12. a   15. a

Something Extra: 800

Page 115

1. 144   100   3. 347   300
2. 919   900   4. 121   100

Page 116

Part 1

1. >   2. >   3. <   4. <   5. >   6. <

Part 2

Answers will vary.

Page 117

1. <   6. <   11. >   16. >   21. >
2. <   7. >   12. <   17. >   22. >
3. >   8. <   13. <   18. <
4. <   9. <   14. <   19. >
5. >   10. >   15. >   20. <

Page 118

1. 20 inches   3. 36 inches
2. 16 inches   4. 20 inches

Page 119

1. b   3. b   5. a   7. b   9. b
2. a   4. b   6. b   8. a   10. b

Page 120

Part 1

1. 1 inch   3. 1 inch   5. 3 inches
2. 2 inches   4. 2 inches

Part 2

Answers will vary.

Page 121

1. b   2. a   3. a   4. b   5. a   6. b

Page 122

1. tea pitcher   3. swimming pool
2. cup of hot chocolate   4. orange juice container

Page 123

1. mL   3. L   5. mL   7. L   9. L
2. L   4. mL   6. mL   8. L   10. mL

Page 124

Part 1

1. a   2. b   3. b   4. a   5. b   6. a

Part 2

Answers will vary.

Page 125

1. c   2. d   3. b   4. c   5. c   6. a

Page 126

1. 9:00   5. 6:30   9. 1:30
2. 7:30   6. 7:00   10. 10:00
3. 2:30   7. 2:00   *Something Extra:*
4. 12:00   8. 8:00

Page 127

Page 128

Part 2

Answers will vary.

Page 129

Part 2

1. cube   2. cone   3. sphere   4. cylinder

Answer Key for Third Grade *(cont.)*

Page 130

1. b   2. c   3. a   4. d

Page 131

Part 1

The following items should be circled: skateboard, computer, party hat.

Part 2

Answers will vary.

Page 132

1. c   2. b   3. a   4. b

Page 133 Answers will vary.

Page 134 Suggested answers.

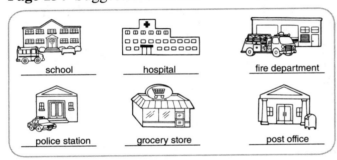

school   hospital   fire department

police station   grocery store   post office

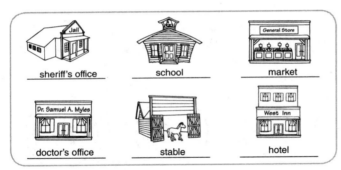

sheriff's office   school   market

doctor's office   stable   hotel

Page 135

Page 136

1. Town Populations
2. Cedar Hill
3. Ashland City and Thomasville
4. Cedar Hill, Pleasant View, Ashland City, and Thomasville
5. Pleasant View; 4,500

6. 3,000

Something Extra: Answers will vary.

Page 137

1. north
2. east
3.

4. Northern, Southern, Western, Eastern
5. Answers will vary.
6. below

Page 138

1. b   2. a   3. b   4. a   5. b

Page 139

1. Vacation Town Map
2. trees
3. mountains
4. yes
5. yes
6. yes
7. Check symbol on the key.
8. Check symbol on the map.

Page 140

1. 10%
2. English
3. German
4. 15%
5. 35%
6. Spanish
7. Italian
8. Answers will vary.

Page 141

1. to state or say something
2. to be free of others
3. Thomas Jefferson
4. The document was written to declare that the colonists of America wanted to be free from England if the King would not listen to them.
5. the War of Independence
6. July 4, 1776

Page 142

1. the Revolutionary War
2. the Constitution
3. that the thirteen colonies wanted to be free from England.
4. what rights Americans would have and how they would live once they were free from England.
5. Answers will vary.

Page 143

1. flag   3. fifty   5. thirteen
2. designs   4. fifty states   6. colonies

Page 144

1. a   2. b   3. a   4. b   5. a

Page 145 Answers will vary.

Answer Key for Third Grade *(cont.)*

Page 146
1. three
2. legislative, executive, and judicial
3. none—the power is divided equally
4. to make sure there was never one person with all the power, like the King of England
5. Answers will vary.

Page 147
1. b   2. a   3. g   4. e   5. f   6. d   7. c

Page 148 Answers will vary.

Page 149

Part 1

Things that need energy from the sun: a plant, a tree, a person, a garden, a solar-powered car

Part 2 Answers will vary.

Page 150
1. gas   3. gas   5. liquid
2. liquid   4. solid   6. solid

Page 151 Answers will vary.

Page 152
1. b   3. c   5. d   7. g   9. i
2. j   4. h   6. e   8. f   10. a

Page 153
1. false   3. true   5. true   7. true
2. false   4. false   6. false   8. true

Something Extra: Check and discuss illustrations.

Page 154
1. pull   3. pull   5. push
2. push   4. push   6. push

Page 155
1. force   2. towards
3. orbit   4. further
5. far away   6. gravity

Page 156
1. b   2. b   3. a   4. b

Page 157 Answers will vary.

Page 158

Part 1 (basic definitions)
1. eat only plants
2. eat only meat
3. eat both plants and meat
4. break down and eat dead plants and animals
5. living things that make their own food
6. living things that cannot make their own food
7. explains how living things get the food they need to make energy

Part 2
1. green plants, corn, acorns, nuts, bark
2. other animals, plants, insects
3. flowers, fresh greens, vegetables, bark

Page 159

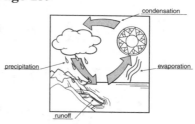

Page 160

Part 1

Answers will vary.

Part 2

 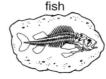

plant   fish   dragonfly

Page 161

Part 1
1. sun   3. axis   5. night
2. Earth   4. day

Part 2

Quarter Moon   **Full Moon**

Page 162

True statements that should be colored:
2. The moon is part of our solar system.
5. The outer planets are farther from the sun.
6. Earth rotates, or spins, on its axis.
8. The moon really doesn't change its shape.

Page 163

Part 1
1. 2   2. Mercury   3. No. It is too hot.

Part 2
1. Neptune   2. Saturn   3. Uranus

Page 164 Answers will vary.

Page 165

Answers will vary, but more sleep seems to equal better grades.

Page 166 Answers will vary.

Page 167 Answers will vary.

Bonus Section

This section offers a jump start for fourth-grade skills in language arts and math for those third-grade students who are ready to move ahead.

Paragraph Writing

Every paragraph starts with a topic sentence. This tells the main idea of the paragraph. Next, there will be several sentences that support this idea. Finally, the last sentence will conclude or sum up the paragraph.

> A dog makes a good pet. (*main idea or topic sentence*) This pet is loyal to its owner. (*supporting sentence*) When you want to play, a dog is always willing to play with you. (*supporting sentence*) A dog will greet you the minute you get home. (*supporting sentence*) These are only a few reasons why a dog makes a fantastic pet. (*concluding sentence*)

Directions: The following sentences from a paragraph about school are all out of order. On your own sheet of paper, rewrite the sentences in order to create a well-written paragraph.

1. Finally, you can learn a lot in school by being a good listener and really listening to what your teacher is saying.

2. School is a wonderful place to learn if you just follow a few simple rules.

3. Next, you should always take notes so that you don't miss any important details the teacher is sharing with the class.

4. Of course, there are many things you can do to learn a lot in school, but just following these simple rules will definitely make a difference on how well you do at school!

5. First, be prepared for class. It's hard to learn if you aren't ready to learn.

Pronouns and Antecedents

A *pronoun* is a word that takes the place of a noun. When a pronoun is used in place of a noun, the noun it takes the place of is called an *antecedent.* It is important to know what the antecedent is to make sure the right type of pronoun is used.

> <u>Jasper</u> wanted to have <u>his</u> birthday party at the bowling alley.

"His" is the pronoun used in the above sentence to take the place of the noun "Jasper." *Jasper* is the antecedent. You would not want to use the pronouns *it, them,* or *her* for the word "Jasper" because then the sentence would not be correct.

Part 1

Directions: Read each sentence. Circle the correct pronoun choice. Underline the antecedent.

1. Jeff went to (its, his) house after school was over.

2. I saw Candy and (her, their) mother at the mall.

3. Michael, do (me, you) know what time the game starts?

4. Sally gave the dog (its, your) treat for the night.

5. Cal wore (his, its) football jersey on the day of the game.

6. Mr. and Mrs. Boyte invited Sandy to (his, their) house for the holidays.

Part 2

Directions: Read each sentence. Then, write the correct pronoun on the line.

1. Tim said I could borrow _____ glove for the baseball game.

2. Mary and Dallas went swimming at _____ grandmother's house.

3. Teresa asked _____ mother for twenty dollars.

Quotation Marks with Titles

If you have a short work, such as a poem, a short story, a chapter in a book, the name of a television episode, or the name of a song, you must do something special to the title. These titles should all be placed inside quotation marks. This lets readers know that what they are reading is actually a title.

> **Example**
>
> My favorite poem "The Rose" is really about the coming of spring and not just about the beautiful flower.

Part 1

Directions: Add quotation marks around the titles wherever they are needed.

1. My favorite chapter in the book is The Hidden Key, which is near the end of the book.

2. Go Home is my favorite song.

3. Have you read the poem Don't Cry by James Kilburn?

4. Last week's episode of How to Lose Weight helped me with my diet.

5. I wish I knew the words to the song My Life by the Amazing Peppers.

6. She read the poem My Puppy and Me to the entire class.

Part 2

Directions: Write titles as described below. Use quotation marks as needed. *Hint:* If you have a literature book, use it to help you find some of the answers.

1. Write the title of a poem you have read:

   _____

2. Write the title of your favorite song:

   _____

3. Write the title of a short story you enjoy:

   _____

Understanding Genre

Writing can be divided into categories or genres. Imagine telling someone what type of movie you like to watch. Maybe you like comedies, or maybe you like horror movies, or maybe you like science fiction. When you divide things into groups, you are dividing them into *genres*. Books can be divided into many different genres. Some of the most popular genres include fairy tales, nonfiction, fiction, fantasies, biography, autobiographies, and historical fiction.

Directions: Match each book title to the correct genre. Write the letter that matches each book title on the line beside it.

____ 1. *My Life* by Abraham Lincoln   **a.** fairy tale

____ 2. *The Story of the Little Pig and the Wicked Witch*   **b.** autobiography

____ 3. *The Complete Guide to Stamp Collecting*   **c.** biography

____ 4. *The Fantastic Voyage to Mercury and Mars*   **d.** fiction

____ 5. *George Washington America's First President* by Tim Ford   **e.** fantasy

     f. nonfiction

____ 6. *The Third Grade Adventures of Tommy Tan*

Idioms

All languages have idioms. Idioms make language fun and interesting. *Idioms* are words or phrases that have a new meaning other than the literal meaning they should have. Does this sound confusing? Then, let's look at it another way.

"A frog in her throat" is an idiom. If you *picture* the words you would imagine a woman with a real frog in her throat. But, an idiom is not understood by its literal meaning. To understand an idiom, you have to consider the other words in the sentence as in, "That woman *talks* like she has a frog in her throat."

Directions: Read each idiom. In the space underneath the idiom, draw a picture of what it seems like the idiom means. Then, write what you think the real definition of the idiom is on the lines.

1. born with a silver spoon in his mouth	**3.** he's all thumbs
2. butterflies in her stomach	**4.** raining cats and dogs

Recognizing Stereotypes

The media often stereotypes certain people. As a savvy viewer, you must be able to tell when people are being stereotyped. No two people are the same. Just because someone likes sports, for example, doesn't mean that he or she can't also like to play chess! Use the exercise below to help recognize stereotyping.

Directions: Below is a picture of a stereotypical superhero. (Notice the long cape, the thick boots, the superhero smile, etc.) In the empty space, draw and color a picture of a superhero who does not have the stereotypical "superhero look." Underneath your picture, list your superhero's strengths and skills. Be prepared to explain to the class why your superhero is better than the one already drawn for you.

My superhero is great because _____

_____

_____

_____

Understanding Morals and Themes

Directions: Read about fables and fiction stories. Then, fill in the blanks below.

Many students are familiar with fables. Fables are fun to read. They are often short stories where the main characters are usually animals. However, the animals or characters usually represent people. At the end of the fable, a short lesson is generally taught to the reader about human nature. Sometimes at the end of a fable there will be a line that states, "And the moral or lesson of the story is . . ." One of the most well-known fables is the story of the tortoise and the hare who have a race. At the end of the story, the reader learns the moral is to never give up because going slow and steady can win the race.

Fiction stories, like fables, are also a lot of fun to read. Fiction stories can also teach the reader a lesson. Unlike fables, there will be no moral written at the end of the story. The reader of a fiction story usually must figure out the lesson from the story that he or she has read. In fiction, this lesson is called the theme or "the universal message." Why is it called the universal message? Well, if a student in China reads the same story as a student in America, the two students might choose the same theme for the book. If both students read a book about a friendship between two boys and both of the main characters had unusual handicaps, the universal message might be that good friends can overcome any problems. The theme does not mention specific characters or settings in a story. It is a general lesson or message about the story. The same theme might even fit more than one story!

Fables are short stories. The main characters are usually _____.

The animals in fables are usually representations of_____.

The lesson at the end of a fable is called the _____ of the story.

Fiction stories also have a similar lesson when a reader is finished with the story.

In a fiction story, the lesson is called the _____.

The definition for theme is the _____.

The theme never mentions specific _____ or _____.

The theme is simply a _____ message about the story. Amazingly,

the same theme just might go with more than one _____!

Division

Part 1

Directions: Find the quotient.

1.

$4\overline{)1{,}768}$

2.

$5\overline{)2{,}525}$

3.

$4\overline{)4{,}828}$

4.

$3\overline{)3{,}339}$

5.

$9\overline{)8{,}181}$

6.

$6\overline{)7{,}218}$

7.

$8\overline{)4{,}872}$

8.

$4\overline{)3{,}292}$

9.

$2\overline{)9{,}212}$

10.

$4\overline{)4{,}488}$

11.

$5\overline{)2{,}530}$

12.

$6\overline{)7{,}626}$

Part 2

Directions: Use division to solve the word problem.

There were 1881 people in the theater. The speaker needed the crowd divided into 9 groups. How many people would be in each group if the people in the theater were divided into 9 equal groups?

Show your work:

Answer:

_____

Using a Calculator

A calculator is a great tool for adding and subtracting once you have mastered the basics of addition and subtraction. Using a calculator just takes some practice.

If you want to add 44 + 55, you should first enter the number 44 into the calculator. Then, hit the "+" (addition) button. Next, enter the number 55. Then, hit the "=" (equals) button. The answer should show up as 99.

To subtract on the calculator, you must also enter the numbers in a certain order. To solve the subtraction problem 99 – 45 on the calculator. first, enter the number 99. Then, hit the "–" (subtraction) button. Next, enter the number 45. Then, hit the "=" (equals) button. The answer should show up as 54.

Directions: Use the following addition and subtraction problems to practice calculator math. Write your answer on the line.

1. 77 – 38 = _____

2. 89 + 34 = _____

3. 92 – 54 = _____

4. 22 + 65 = _____

5. 76 – 22 = _____

6. 12 + 34 = _____

7. 63 – 25 = _____

8. 45 + 54 = _____

9. 88 – 42 = _____

10. 18 + 77 = _____

11. 34 – 23 = _____

12. 41 + 52 = _____

13. 94 – 48 = _____

14. 34 + 21 = _____

15. 49 – 33 = _____

16. 39 + 38 = _____

Perfecting Patterns

When you complete a pattern, you are finding out what happens next.

Directions: Complete each pattern below.

1. △, △, ○, ○, □, □, △, _____, _____

2. 10, 20, 30, 40, _____, _____, _____

3. 1, 3, 5, 7, _____, _____, _____

4. ☆, ♡, ☆, ○, _____, □

5. 2, 4, 8, 16, 32, _____

6. 55, 44, 33, 22, _____

7. ZYX, WVU, TSR, _____, _____, _____

8. dog, puppy, cat, kitten, cow, _____

9. Apple, Ball, Cake, Dog, Egg, _____

10. Q, D, N, Q, D, _____, _____

11. Andy, Bill, Cal, David, Evan, Frank, _____, _____

12. 99, 98, 89, 88, 79, _____, _____, _____

Something Extra: Create a pattern of your own. See if a classmate can complete the pattern you created.

Geometry

An *angle* is two rays with a common end point. The *vertex* is the name of the common end point. A *right angle* is an angle that forms a square corner. Its measurement is 90 degrees.

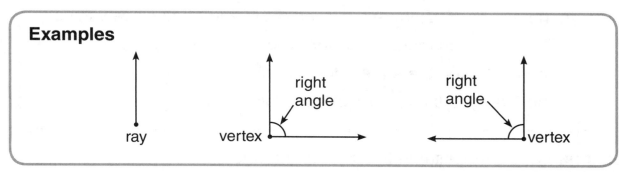

Examples

ray   vertex   right angle   right angle   vertex

Part 1

Directions: Practice finding right angles. Think about some of the things in or around your desk. Just by looking at the items, you will find right angles. Write down the examples you find.

Example: The corner of a textbook is a right angle. It forms a square corner.

1. _____

2. _____

3. _____

4. _____

Part 2

Directions: Look at each figure. Write "R" if the figure is a right angle. Write "No" if the figure is not a right angle.

1. _____

2. _____

3. _____

4. _____

5. _____

6. _____

Place Value

Three-digit numbers are made up of three place values.

> **Example**
>
> In the number **527**, there are three digits and three place values.
>
> The 5 tells you there are **5 hundreds** in this number.
>
> The 2 tells you there are **2 tens** in this number.
>
> The 7 tell you there are **7 ones** in this number.

Directions: Circle the letter of the correct answer.

1.   **789**
 The number 8 is in the ___ place.
    a. ones
    b. tens
    c. hundreds
	5. **578**
	 The number 7 is in the ___ place.
	    a. ones
	    b. tens
	    c. hundreds

2.   **290**
 The number 2 is in the ___ place.
    a. ones
    b. tens
    c. hundreds
	6. **988**
	 The number 9 is in the ___ place.
	    a. ones
	    b. tens
	    c. hundreds

3.   **891**
 The number 1 is in the ___ place.
    a. ones
    b. tens
    c. hundreds
	7. **645**
	 The number 4 is in the ___ place.
	    a. ones
	    b. tens
	    c. hundreds

4.   **327**
 The number 3 is in the ___ place.
    a. ones
    b. tens
    c. hundreds
	8. **296**
	 The number 6 is in the ___ place.
	    a. ones
	    b. tens
	    c. hundreds

Finding the Mean or Average

The *mean* of a group of numbers is sometimes called the average of the numbers. To find the mean, you must add all of the numbers in the group and divide by the total amount of numbers.

Example

$$
\begin{array}{r}
19 \\
20 \\
17 \\
+\ 40 \\
\hline
96
\end{array}
$$

$96 \div 4 = 24$ **Mean** $= 24$

Directions: Find the mean of each set of numbers.

1. 171, 187, 376, 221, 100 **Mean** _____	**5.** 555, 601 **Mean** _____
2. 777, 238, 998, 631 **Mean** _____	**6.** 789, 712, 444, 871 **Mean** _____
3. 263, 258, 298 **Mean** _____	**7.** 444, 489, 431, 490, 435, 459 **Mean** _____
4. 192, 171, 134, 190, 123 **Mean** _____	**8.** 321, 398, 103 **Mean** _____

Subtracting Money

When you subtract with decimals, the decimal does not change position. This is especially important if you are subtracting amounts of money. You would not want the amount of money to change because you accidentally moved a decimal.

Directions: Solve the following subtraction problems.

1. $77.23
       − $23.12

8. $87.98
       − $23.21

2. $23.91
       − $11.81

9. $65.43
       − $52.22

3. $18.12
       − $12.10

10. $39.37
       − $27.16

4. $57.23
       − $43.11

11. $44.19
       − $17.02

5. $67.79
       − $33.28

12. $19.19
       − $12.02

6. $34.98
       − $22.66

13. $72.27
       − $22.14

7. $98.12
       − $77.09

14. $29.23
       − $13.13

Answer Key for Bonus Section

Page 177

(2) School is a wonderful place to learn if you just follow a few simple rules. (5) First, be prepared for class. It's hard to learn if you aren't ready to learn. (3) Next, you should always take notes so that you don't miss any important details the teacher is sharing with the class. (1) Finally, you can learn a lot in school by being a good listener and really listening to what your teacher is saying. (4) Of course, there are many things you can do to learn a lot in school, but just following these simple rules will definitely make a difference on how well you do at school!

Page 178

Part 1

1. his	Jeff
2. her	Candy
3. you	Michael
4. its	dog
5. his	Cal
6. their	Mr. and Mrs. Boyte

Part 2

1. his
2. their
3. her

Page 179

Part 1

1. "The Hidden Key"
2. "Go Home"
3. "Don't Cry"
4. "How to Lose Weight"
5. "My Life"
6. "My Puppy and Me"

Part 2

Answers will vary.

Page 180

1. b
2. a
3. f
4. e
5. c
6. d

Page 181

Answers will vary but may be similar to:

1. He has everything.
2. She is nervous.
3. He is clumsy.
4. It is raining a lot.

Page 182

Answers will vary.

Page 183

Fables are short stories. The main characters are usually <u>animals</u>. The animals in fables are usually representations of <u>humans/people</u>. The lesson at the end of a fable is called the <u>moral</u> of the story.

Fiction stories also have a similar lesson when a reader is finished with the story. In a fiction story, the lesson is called the <u>theme</u>. The definition for theme is the <u>universal</u> <u>message</u>. The theme never mentions specific <u>characters</u> or <u>settings</u>. The theme is simply a <u>general</u> message about the story. Amazingly, the same theme just might go with more than one <u>story</u>!

Page 184

Part 1

1. 442
2. 505
3. 1207
4. 1113
5. 909
6. 1203
7. 609
8. 823
9. 4606
10. 1122
11. 506
12. 1271

Part 2

209 people

Answer Key for Bonus Section *(cont.)*

Page 185

1. 39
2. 123
3. 38
4. 87
5. 54
6. 46
7. 38
8. 99
9. 46
10. 95
11. 11
12. 93
13. 46
14. 55
15. 16
16. 77

Page 186

1. △ , ○
2. 50, 60, 70
3. 9, 11, 13
4. ☆
5. 64
6. 11
7. QPO, NML, KJI
8. calf
9. Answers will vary, but it must be a noun that starts with the letter "f."
10. Ⓝ , Ⓠ
11. Answers will vary, but it must be a boy's name that starts with the letter "G."
12. 78, 69, 68

Something Extra: Answers will vary.

Page 187

Part 1

Answers will vary.

Part 2

1. R
2. No
3. R
4. No
5. R
6. No

Page 188

1. b
2. c
3. a
4. c
5. b
6. c
7. b
8. a

Page 189

1. 211
2. 661
3. 273
4. 162
5. 578
6. 704
7. 458
8. 274

Page 190

1. $54.11
2. $12.10
3. $6.02
4. $14.12
5. $34.51
6. $12.32
7. $21.03
8. $64.77
9. $13.21
10. $12.21
11. $27.17
12. $7.17
13. $50.13
14. $16.10